Design for Sports

THE CULT OF PERFORMANCE

Design
for
Sports

THE CULT OF
PERFORMANCE

Edited by Akiko Busch

**Cooper-Hewitt
National Design Museum
Smithsonian Institution
and
Princeton Architectural Press**

PUBLISHED BY

Princeton Architectural Press

37 East Seventh Street

New York, NY 10003

02 01 00 99 98   5 4 3 2 1

FIRST EDITION

PROJECT COORDINATOR: Mark Lamster

COVER AND BOOK DESIGN: Sara E. Stemen

Special thanks to Eugenia Bell, Caroline Green, Clare Jacobson,
Therese Kelly, and Annie Nitschke of Princeton Architectural Press
                              —Kevin C. Lippert, publisher

Printed and bound in China

For a free catalog of books published by Princeton Architectural
Press, call toll free 1.800.722.6657 or visit www.papress.com

LIBRARY OF CONGRESS CATALOGING-IN-PUBLICATION DATA

Design for Sports / edited by Akiko Busch. — 1st ed.

       p. cm.

    Includes bibliographical references

    ISBN 1-56898-145-7 (alk. paper)

       1. Sporting goods—United States   I. Busch, Akiko. II.

Cooper-Hewitt Museum.

    GV745.D47 1998

688.7'0973—dc21   97-36554

                                                       CIP

COVER PHOTOGRAPHS:

TOP: courtesy Nike Inc.

BOTTOM: golf putters courtesy USGA, Far Hills, NJ

Contents

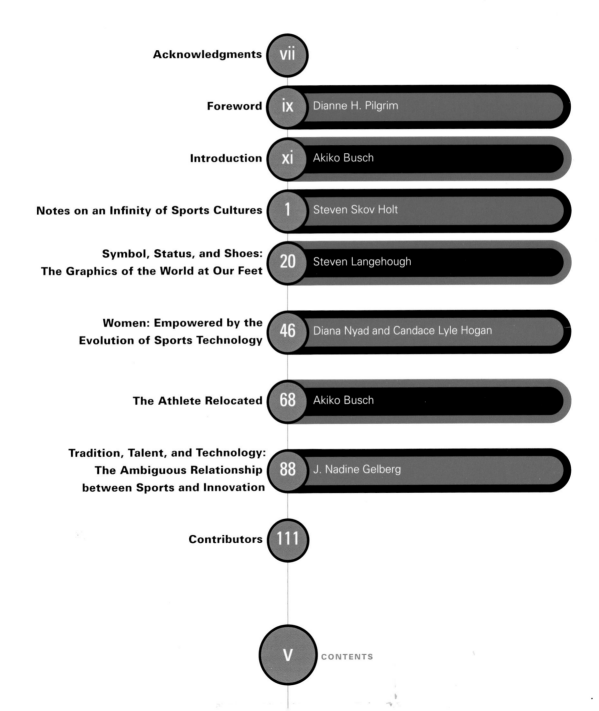

Acknowledgments

CONTEMPORARY SPORTS ARE OFTEN about vertical challenges—mountain bikes speedracing down steep grades or rock climbers scaling precipitous heights. This work has offered its own sequence of vertical challenges, and I am grateful to the many who have helped me maneuver those inclines.

Thanks are due foremost to the authors who contributed to this collection—from the start Candace Lyle Hogan, Steven Skov Holt, J. Nadine Gelberg, and Diana Nyad brought their own perspectives, experience, and intelligence to this book, and I am grateful for these immeasurable contributions. I am especially thankful to Steven Langehough, my collaborator at the National Design Museum. His reliable insights, unerring ability to ask just the right questions at the right time, steady nerves, and steadfast dry wit served to keep us all focused throughout. Thanks are due as well to Mark Lamster of Princeton Architectural Press, whose comment and final edit—delivered within a brutally short period of time—have proven essential, and to Sara Stemen for her thoughtful and spirited design.

At Cooper-Hewitt, National Design Museum, thanks go to Dianne Pilgrim first for inviting me to participate in this project; and then to Susan Yelavich for her continuing support, encouragement, and conviction that sports objects speak to our cultural identity; to Ellen Lupton for her thoughtful insights; to Sheri Sandler for her persistent efforts and stamina in securing the means to publish this book; to Caroline Mortimer for helping to transform a sequence of ideas into a finished document; to Jeff McCartney for sage editorial counsel; to Christine McKee and Yanitza Tavarez for early voluminous research; to Krista Connerly for her patient and thorough work in managing seemingly unmanageable volumes of material; to Tracy Myers for patience and support throughout; and to Kim Brandt for her tireless work in obtaining photographs and permissions. I am grateful as well to Mike Mills, whose insights were at the genesis of this project.

Thanks as well to Michael Beirut at Pentagram for his shrewd eye and clear focus; and to James Biber at Pentagram for good humor, creative counsel, and for the other assorted cups of psychic Gatorade along the way.

Akiko Busch

Foreword

Dianne H. Pilgrim, Director
Cooper-Hewitt, National Design Museum

THE CULTURE OF SPORTS engages us as avid viewers and knowledgeable consumers in a form of national theater. This work sets out to examine those ways in which design is a lively—indeed essential—player in this theater.

Historians of design have traditionally treated the artifacts of sport as either objects of science or objects of sculpture. To be sure, both are valid approaches. New technologies, new materials, and human kinesthetics intersect with grace and energy in the study of sports science. Similarly, the inventive form and graphics of much of this new equipment legitimizes its study in purely aesthetic terms.

But it is the intent of this volume to look at sports equipment not simply as objects of art or science, but as persuasive documents of contemporary culture. Insofar as the ordinary objects of everyday life reflect our needs, our desires, our national character at large, so then can a hockey mask, bicycle frame, or snowboard reveal facets of our cultural identity. While a basketball shoe may enable a player to jump higher, it may also serve as a potent expression of personal identity. A machine-made soccer ball may suggest an increasing sensitivity to ethical issues of Third World labor, while synthetic climbing walls suggest a radically revised relationship to the natural world. These concerns are central to the mission of the Cooper-Hewitt, National Design Museum, which seeks to explore the complex relationship of design to everyday life.

The study of design is, so often, the study of the relationship between people and things. In the realm of sports, that relationship is, by nature, lively, dynamic, and energetic. Indeed, the very nature of sports equipment makes it among the most tested and documented products of design. These essays set out to document that energy. And just as digital cameras monitor the runner's speed at the finish line down to the millisecond, just as an accelerometer inside a punching bag calculates exactly the force of the boxer's punch, so does this work set out to record and reflect upon those less quantifiable values that the artifacts of sport suggest we hold as a society.

I am grateful to editor Akiko Busch and Steven Langehough, her partner on this project at the National Design Museum, for their enthusiasm and diligence. Their comprehensive understanding of a broad and complex topic allowed them to focus this study on some of the most fascinating manifestations of design today: sports equipment. I also thank Sheri Sandler for her dedicated efforts in raising the funds to make this book possible. The National Design Museum acknowledges the critical support of Condé Nast/Sports for Women and The Sara Lee Foundation for their early support for this project.

Introduction

Akiko Busch

O BJECTS, LIKE PEOPLE, can live double lives. And contemporary sports equipment thrives—with subtlety, wit, and pure exuberance—on its rich double life. The new materials and technology of such equipment have redefined the way sports are played, enhancing speed, force, distance, height. At the same time, however, their forms spell out clearly and consistently our cultural profile. For all the energy and vitality this equipment represents, what it may do with the greatest agility and grace is serve these two functions at once.

Sports—and sports figures—engage our cultural imagination because they thrive in an arena in which human physical ability and technology intersect precisely, powerfully, and gracefully. Whereas elsewhere in modern life technology may be perceived as overpowering or in some way capable of diminishing the human, in the realm of sports it is empowering. Stronger, more durable, and more lightweight materials—such as Kevlar, titanium, graphite, and assorted other fiber-reinforced composites—are reshaping sports equipment. Oversized tennis rackets, double-kicktail skateboards, parabolic skis, and reconfigured golf clubs have all changed the very nature of their respective sports, setting new standards of technical performance and what the human body can accomplish.

Perhaps more than any other category of artifact, sports equipment underscores the fact that design—the form and material of physical objects—has increased the potential for human physical ability.

At the same time, however, these artifacts serve as metaphors for our cultural values. The shatterproof, thermoplastic face mask used by hockey goalies, hand-painted with the image of a Bengal tiger, has a threatening quality that serves as its own psychological weapon; the helmet outfitted with a video camera efficiently films the maneuvers of sky surfers; that a sport can be fully appreciated both by the athlete and spectator only once it has been recorded on film suggests an intersection of self-reflection and performance that is truly modern. Both of these articles of headgear have a symbolic content that supplements their technical performance. Indeed, as sports artifacts become reshaped, they have also become increasingly potent symbols expressing a variety of societal and cultural themes.

Consider, for example, the hybrid nature of contemporary sports equipment. Whereas skates, skis, and surfboards all developed independently in a relatively linear manner, board sports today are more changeable, thriving on appropriation. In-line skates, skateboards, airboards, snowboards, wakeboards, street luge boards, and snow skates—all of these pieces of equipment—and the cultures they represent—beg, borrow, and steal from one another in a fluid exchange that is purely contemporary.

Indeed, all of these different board sports are capable of morphing into one another with the same agility and grace of the athletes maneuvering them. What makes this relevant, of course, is that elsewhere in our lives we have come to accept the notion that identity is fluid. That the self can be reinvented is a conventional wisdom of the times; ours is a culture that celebrates transformation— and the faster it can be made, the better. We resculpt our bodies at health clubs and gyms, and the advent in recent years of "esthetic surgery" demonstrates the appeal of physical metamorphosis at the hands of the surgeon. Tattoos, body piercing, and other assorted graphics of the human body have rarely held out the popular appeal they do today. Just as the exterior self can be redefined, the interior self can be reconfigured as well with any selection from a host of modern therapies. If we were introduced a generation ago to the notion that the nature of reality might be shifted with mind-altering and illegal drugs, our ready use today of such prescribed medications as Prozac suggests that we accept the idea that the chemistry of the brain—and the behavior it generates—can be easily amended. That the appeal of personal reinvention has reached an all time high is reflected further in children's literature. A favored series of books among young children today is *Anamorphs*, by K. A. Applegate. Throughout the series, children are morphed into creatures of all sorts—eagles, bears, and tigers—all of which transform their identities and abilities, imbuing them with new powers in the process.

As Steven Skov Holt points out, the culture of sports reflects our ease in morphing (or perhaps our need to morph). In his essay exploring the theme of fluidity, "Notes on an Infinity of Sports Cultures," he writes:

> Change is fun, it's easy to do, and it's in synch with the way things are in life. Since it's going to happen anyway, why not ride it, surf it, play it, and make it part of sport? Whereas earlier generations embraced a more rooted lifestyle (growing up in the same community) and rooted workstyle (staying employed at the same company), the new generation welcomes diversity, variety, flexibility. For this reason alone, the new generation of sports equipment is some of the most fluid and accommodating gear yet devised for any human activity.

If our identity is capable of taking on these myriad guises, how we express them is no less significant. Steven Langehough observes that the shoe has always been a symbol of identity, capable of conveying us to an assortment of different psychic landscapes. The photoessay he has assembled here investigates how the contemporary athletic shoe serves as an especially compelling vehicle of self-expression. As he observes, "If the automobile captured the popular imagination of the fifties, symbolizing the new prosperity of that time, today the athletic shoe has become a more democratic symbol of identity and prestige in multicultural America."

The identities of the individual, of the team, and of the street subculture are frequently spelled out by the graphics of shoes and how they are worn—laced or unlaced for example, tied or untied. Langehough tours a variety of sports subcultures, focusing on how they are revealed through the graphics of their shoes, using images of sports equipment as well as the language and graphics of sports commercials and marketing programs. He also examines the emerging roles of the woman athlete and how the graphics of athletic footwear and marketing reflect evolving perceptions of women in society.

Former marathon swimmer Diana Nyad and journalist Candace Lyle Hogan reflect further upon the emerging role of women in sports as seen through the lens of equipment and apparel. If the development of sports technology has represented speed and strength and sometimes safety for men, for women it has signaled freedom. Higher achievements in athleticism and growing public acceptance have together empowered women athletes and led to the heightened visibility of women's sports. Increasingly lightweight equipment has also made some women's sports faster and therefore more appealing to spectators. That the 1996 Olympics were dubbed the Women's Olympics, that the WNBA and ABL—competing women's professional basketball leagues—enjoyed widely celebrated inaugural seasons in 1997, and that a number of new sports magazines published exclusively for the woman athlete have been introduced in the last several years all suggest we have entered a golden age for the sportswoman.

Nyad and Hogan, however, provide a historical perspective for this change, pointing out that a previous golden age for the female athlete occurred in the late nineteenth century, and they suggest that the diminished role of the American sportswoman in the following decades tells its own social and political story. They also address how contemporary sports equipment continues to acknowledge and address the growing numbers of women who take their sports seriously—and reflect as well upon those areas in which the equipment fails to recognize the emerging woman athlete.

How we, as occupants of the late twentieth century, view the natural world, is reflected in the changing playing field of sports. Our relationship with nature, it seems, is in transition. Traditionally, we have played our sports outdoors. Today, however, fitness machines, indoor golf, and a whole realm of virtual sports equipment all relocate—and at times dislocate—the athlete. Wave machines can be installed in swimming pools to create "a surf;"

golf clubs can be reassembled as shafts of light; towers of ice cooled by liquid nitrogen can be sculpted into vertical speed climbing walls without the extremes of wind and temperature associated with conventional alpine climbing; we can breathe thin mountain air in urban fitness spas and ride bikes on traffic-free video monitors. All of these would suggest an estrangement from the conditions of nature, conditions that were once integrally connected to the practice of sport.

In sports, the synthetic realm may be safer, more entertaining, more egalitarian. It offers us more choices and more control. In sport and in life alike, nature, it seems, is no longer a governing condition, but simply a component in modern experience. And insofar as the artifacts of the physical world are documents of civilization, the sports equipment we use today reaffirms a broader cultural view that the natural world is, if not disposable, then certainly negotiable.

In her essay on tradition and technology, J. Nadine Gelberg examines how our cultural ambivalence toward new technologies is expressed and handled in the realm of sports. While titanium bats, diamond-coated golf clubs, and assorted other space-age materials may give the impression that sports embrace technological innovation, the truth is that sports organizations regularly prohibit creative new designs in their efforts to preserve sporting tradition. By examining the role of tradition in the design of sports equipment, focusing in particular on the design of tennis rackets, golf balls, baseball bats, and bicycles, Gelberg suggests that nostalgia and a tenacious hold on sporting tradition—rather than performance—still govern the design of some equipment.

Gelberg observes that technological innovation has frequently compromised both the sporting

challenge and the traditions of games, and catalogs a variety of sports equipment that, while enhancing performance, also transforms the nature of a sport in ways that are deemed unacceptable. How advances in technology may compromise tradition and how we choose to accept or reject these compromises are, of course, larger questions we routinely face as occupants of the millennium.

The equipment of sports engages our cultural imagination. But it also engages us because we find ourselves increasingly engaged in a world of immateriality. The appeal of the intangible realm is growing on us—whether it is in the anonymous exchanges of cyberspace, the competitive environment of an on-line game, or the professional affiliations we may find in an Internet community. No surprise, then that we also look to the very physicality of sport to balance these out. If we seek our identity on Web sites, of course we must look for it as well on the soccer field and the basketball court. For all the abstract, intangible benefits offered to us by contemporary electronic technology, we long as well to be satisfied and nourished by the physical realm—to touch, hold, catch, throw. And therein lies the enduring appeal of contemporary sports.

As these authors observe, the equipment of sports serves as a clear lens for broader societal issues. The new materials and technology of sports are indeed empowering. Parabolic or sidecut skis, introduced on the market only a few years ago, have redefined skiing, giving users a new degree of control and precision in carving mountain trails. A ten-ounce Kevlar bike helmet can save a biker's life. Soft boots bring the casual comfort and style of a basketball shoe to in-line skates. High-performance fabric gives swimmers a virtual second skin, allowing them to shave seconds off their lap times. All of this equipment and material surely empowers the athletes who use them. But what they may empower us to do most of all is recognize ourselves.

Design for Sports

THE CULT OF PERFORMANCE

Notes on an Infinity of Sports Cultures

STEVEN SKOV HOLT

The Personal Meaning of Sports, Part One

WHEN I WAS ELEVEN and still lived on a Connecticut cul-de-sac named Freedom Drive, the pace of life was so slow and the town so removed from the inner-city maelstroms of the late sixties that we could play ball in the road from the time we got up to the time we went to sleep, and on many days and nights, we did just that. Occasionally, cars would drive through, and we'd glare reflexively at them, but within seconds we'd be back into our games, immersed in the all-enveloping realm of two-on-two touch football, left-handed wiffle ball, street hockey, four square, or ultimate Frisbee.

In those days, my design interests focused on the sports posters my friends and I had on our bedroom walls. If memory serves, amidst the pages torn from *Sports Illustrated*, I had two large posters, one of Reggie Smith, the other of Hank Aaron. Both were baseball players, and both were outfielders. One was local (Boston), the other not (Atlanta). Why them? Because of the way that they played ball. The way that they stood. The way that they moved. The way that they were. They were great at what they did, and I not only responded to them, I wanted to *be* them.

Looking back, I'd have to say my reaction evolved from a combination of factors: my own sense of striving against continual failure along with my realization that Smith and Aaron had a hold on something that 99 percent of the adults I knew had failed to grasp. Simply put, they were doing something they liked. *Something that*

mattered. I decided that the lesson of sports wasn't necessarily to be an athlete—it was to do something you really wanted to do because then you could be good at it.

It wasn't until I was twelve that I realized a more obvious significance to the Smith and Aaron posters: both were African-American. In the aforementioned suburban Connecticut town, families of color were rarely seen. Yet photos of black athletes dominated my wall and the walls of my friends. If not Aaron and Smith at my house, then Frank Robinson at Dave's, Walt Frazier and Connie Hawkins at Michael's, and Lew Alcindor at someone else's. For us, racial integration came by way of televised sports, not by bus. We watched to see who was good, and based on that, decided not only who to root for, but who we wanted to be like.

The Personal Meaning of Sports, Part Two

Around the same time, I also came to believe that my body's physical position as a spectator—the way that I sat, stood, or lay—could influence any game's outcome. Through an intense trial-and-error process, I discovered that my ability to affect a game was directly proportional to how much I cared about the outcome: my favorite team might lose as a result of my crooked elbow or crossed pant leg.

Looking back, I see it as a kind of cosmic ripple effect. Without thinking, I might make a slight, seemingly meaningless movement. Then, almost instantly, something disastrous would occur—an error, a fumble, a turnover, or a dropped pass for my team, or a home run, a goal, a dunk, or a touchdown by the opposition. I'd realize what I had caused, and since I couldn't reverse it, I'd try to divine the next optimal position for my body and move into it.

Years later, when I read about chaos theory, I recognized this as a variant of what author James Gleick called "The Butterfly Effect," the "notion that a butterfly stirring the air today in Peking can transform storm systems next month in New York."[1] I continually chased an ever-evolving rule set in which my clothes and body were equipment for an increasingly convoluted and obsessive mental athletics where what appeared inconsequential and random was, in act, guaranteed to be the opposite. If sports brought out positive traits in me and generated a sensitivity to race, it also brought out such tendencies as this profoundly superstitious, even neurotic, behavior not strictly accountable for by being raised in the WASP environs of rural New England.

In sports, as in life, we can't help but think in terms of what others have done before us. The sculptor Alberto Giacometti said of his contemporaries that although they could look outside, they could see the landscape only in terms of what the painter Camille Pissarro had done; William S. Burroughs has said that after looking at sunflowers painted by Vincent van Gogh, he could never see nature in the same way again.

The power that such imagery has over us is immense. It was thought to be physically impossible for a human to run a sub-four minute mile—until Roger Bannister finally did it in the early fifties. And being thus liberated to do it, dozens of other athletes accomplished this feat within the next year. Such stories offer us a rare insight into the process of how we can exceed our limits; they demonstrate how what we think influences what we can do, see,

experience. It wasn't until I was able to dispel the imagined connection between my own actions and those on the screen that I was able to enjoy watching sports on television.

Thinking About Sports at the End of the Twentieth Century

It wasn't so long ago that we thought of sports as what kids did in their spare time and what adults did if they couldn't grow up. Today, however, we're more likely to consider sports a global form of big business. The direct and indirect sports economy generated by Nike, for example, is larger than that of many states and nations.

Sports haven't been "just sports" for some time. We have more types of sports, sports equipment, and sports participants than any social theorist, scientist, or visionary ever imagined. The full flowering of what social theorist Thorstein Veblein called the "leisure class" is manifested today in entire demographic groups devoted to conspicuously consuming exercises, activities, and sundry accessories. This new breed—call it the Lycra class—sees spare time and vacations as the opportunity to participate in a series of perspiration-infused activities, one following the other in rapid-fire succession.

If we step back for a moment and look at the products that support this phenomenon, it's clear that many of them succeed on multiple levels. These products are different from the banal necessities of everyday life. Their message is one of optimism and positive democratic participation: anyone who's good enough can excel, and excel to the point where they can leave their surroundings behind, literally and figuratively. No hick town, ghetto, or cul-de-sac can hold someone so empowered. In such a way, sports products enable those with kinesthetic intelligence—the kind measured in the field instead of the classroom—to believe that they can surmount the obstacles that birth and environment have otherwise thrown them.

The actual objects of play and the various accessories upon which all sports are founded have changed enormously in the last twenty years. Sure, we still fling, tap, or slap balls into various goals, holes, and nets, but sports equipment also serves as the key prop in the larger drama that sporting events have become. This equipment— shoes, boards, gloves, bats, clothes, souvenirs—has achieved mythological status among youth everywhere precisely because of its promise of liberation and the attendant multimodal media spectacle that celebrates it.

The spectacle of sport—with contemporary protagonists in the age-old drama of competition— creates events of such size, scale, scope, and stature that they are essentially without peer in contemporary culture. For viewers—at the track, stadium, or television—today's sporting events stretch the limits of cognitive information processing by challenging our capacity to absorb it all. There's the action on the field, the incessant music between plays, the various cheerleaders and mascots, the announcers, and the various media streams provided by scoreboards, airborne banners, radios, and hand-held televisions. And far from being an unpleasant visual or aural overload, this excess of information is what we have come to expect; it is essential to the experience of sports. On the various fields of athletic dreams, quietude is no longer an option; every facet in the flow of spectator experience is carefully designed.

Consider that in 1993 the NCAA introduced a day-glo yellow softball with glazed red stitching both because it looked better on camera and was

ABOVE: **Fox Trax Hockey Puck (1996).** The size and speed of the traditional hockey puck make it difficult for viewers to follow on TV. In an effort to build its fan base, Fox Sports developed the Fox Trax, an electronically enhanced puck. Both the length and color of its comet-like tail can be adjusted. Courtesy Fox Sports

RIGHT: **NCAA Optic Yellow Softball (1992).** Wilson introduced this softball in 1993 to help make the televised game a more dynamic and energetic spectacle. Courtesy Wilson Sporting Goods

more visible to spectators in the stands. ESPN had said that it wanted to see more action, and the livelier ball was born, complete with a polyurethane core for extra punch. Major League Baseball also "redesigned" its ball in a transparent attempt to woo back fans with an instant office, home-run blitz to counter the more mediagenic properties of NBA basketball, NFL football, and NHL hockey. Many sports have used technology to further engage existing viewers and to entice new ones. Witness the "comet puck" sponsored by the Fox network: an electronic sensor installed in a hockey puck allows it to produce a red, cometlike tail when

> Our sports gear suggests the possibility of corporeal escape—a kind of psychic involvement with something far larger, more powerful, and more perfect than any one of us could reasonably hope to be a part of.

filmed on camera. Similarly, the in-car and on-bike NASCAR, Formula One, and Grand Prix cameras animate the viewers' experience by allowing them to get inside the race car or on the motorcycle.

Then there are the logos. Logos are everywhere—fertile explosions of color and type dotting the athletic landscape. Whether applied to the products or worn by the athletes, logos no longer just sit there waiting for the eyeballs to come to them. Now the logos go after the eyeballs; they race, animate, and graphically collide with one another at breakneck visual speed, and their aggressiveness in seeking attention is matched only by their precise placement on body, equipment, or playing surface. Such logos offer us the opportunity to observe how sports graphics have chucked the standard corporate identity manual out the window, taking product imagery to a whole new level—that of the hyper-iconographic brand where the exterior of many products is transformed into a carefully composed marketing collage.

Nike practices this proactive brand architecture with particular effectiveness, building layer upon layer of exquisitely designed motifs. The company creates a multimedia mass of graphics-in-motion that operates consciously and uncon-

sciously in a way heretofore unknown. Everything from in-your-face advertising to the total Nike Town environment is designed in an effort to transform consumer skepticism to Swoosh loyalty.

As sports continue to occupy center stage in our global culture, its equipment continues to change from nonstylized works of functional folk art to lab-based, fully ergonomic, runway-inspired works of creative abandon, capable of captivating us as no other products can. Sports products of the late nineties express the self-accessorization of our lives and the emergence of the occasional athlete; weekend warriors now possess an array of equipment once reserved for the elite level of world-class athletes. Such professionalization of equipment suggests that our products, for the first time in history, possess abilities far in advance of our own. The absolute high-end, let-it-all-hang-out gear designed for the world champion or gold medalist is now available to anyone off the street with a gold card. Just as many of us now cook at home with sophisticated restaurant equipment, weekend athletes of all types now invest thousands of dollars and impressive amounts of psychic energy in achieving minuscule but highly meaningful competitive advantages over their sports cohorts.

While the obvious way to consider sports equipment is either as a technologic icon or as an artifact of material culture, a more interesting way to think of it may be as a prosthetic in the process of becoming an orthotic. A prosthetic is cloaked in the language of the missing limb; it is based on absence, an inferior and artificial replacement for the real thing. It is attached to us rather than integrated with us. By contrast, the orthotic is a customized product that fuses with the body and encourages a more complete sense of mastery. In sports design, the model of the prosthetic is the past, the orthotic the future. Eventually, many athletic products, starting initially at the higher end, will be reorganized around a custom-produced component supported by a mass-produced shell, structure, or exoskeleton.

These kinds of changes suggest that we have entered into a new type of relationship with our equipment. Our sports gear suggests the possibility of corporeal escape—a kind of psychic involvement with something far larger, more powerful, and more perfect than any one of us could reasonably hope to be a part of. In a way, it fulfills some of the social promises for personal growth manifested in the fifties and sixties. The fact that it has done this so well probably means that some kind of backlash is inevitable, and indeed it has come—strongly, visibly, predictably—in the form of an aggressive punkification of sports. The effect has been to attitudinalize, hybridize, and radicalize existing sports, as well as to invent new ones. In all of this, design has played a key role.

Learning from MTV

Sports are a lot like music; teams are like bands, stadiums are like concert halls, and superstars are a lot like, well, superstars. Sports and music don't simply borrow from one another; they have entire subcultures that seem to migrate back and forth across ever-finer demographic and market lines. Sports and music are both global methods of communication for youth culture (various artists, for example, have called rap the CNN of the inner city because it tells everyone what's up.) The resident site for rap, rock-and-roll, heavy metal, alternative, and techno, a place with its own sports show—and the place that has done the most to make the music

that we hear visible—is MTV. In its heterogeneous mix of styles, brands, lifestyles, and identities, the music network offers a compelling lesson on the fluid nature of contemporary identity.

MTV's corporate identity has used the same system for a number of years: A big, blocky *M* and a smaller, script *TV*. What makes the MTV corporate identity so radically different from other corporate logos is that it thrives on change. Since the beginning, its graphics have been in motion. One day, it's image is the hood of a car, the next a squirt of paint, then state-of-the-art animation, then a celebrity impostor. Elsewhere in corporate America, identity tends to be static, but at MTV, it's never the same thing twice, though it's always the same thing over time. The changeability of the logo is incessant, the *lingua franca* of the whole system.

A similar propensity for movement is hardwired into contemporary sports culture, from the mobility of free agency in professional athletics to the incredible proliferation of sneaker styles to the cross-pollination between road bicycling, mountain bicycling, BMXing, vert ramping, low-riding, and retrofitted cruising. Because sports are all over the airwaves, we'll be seeing a lot more of the I'll-take-a-little-of-this-and-a-little-of-that approach to making things. MTV heralds the ascendancy of a new, pluralistic youth aesthetic, a way of seeing the world based on hybrid thinking, on the newly appreciated beauty of multiracial children, and on the emerging sense that what might have been called confusion or chaos a decade ago is what constitutes beauty today.

Although music is central to the culture of sports, the real lesson from music, courtesy of MTV, is that change is fun, it's easy to do, and it's in synch with the way thing are in life. Since it's going to happen anyway, why not ride it, surf it, play it, and make it part of sport? Whereas earlier generations embraced a more rooted lifestyle (growing up in the same community) and workstyle (staying employed at the same company), the new generation welcomes diversity, variety, flexibility. For this reason alone, the new generation of sports equipment is some of the most fluid and accommodating gear yet devised for *any* human activity.

Radical Golf? Who Would Have Believed It!

Golf offers one of the most compelling examples of just how much things have changed. While golf has long been a popular sport—witness Arnie's Army—who could have predicted that 30,000 viewers of every size, shape, and color would line up at the seventeenth hole of the U.S. Open. In recent years, golf has been removed from the club, repatterned, and turned upside down and inside out by a new generation of players, fans, and designers.

Two events stand out especially regarding golf's new spirit. One is Tiger Woods' introduction to the links of a new, multi-ethnic, hybridized model for what athletic excellence could be, and as significantly, look like. It was an image instantly recognized and promoted by Nike, which signed Woods and ran a television commercial for several months that powerfully captured the sport's new demographic ambitions: youth of all shapes, colors, and backgrounds were filmed, saying "I am Tiger Woods." In much the same way that Andre Agassi shattered the Wimbledon ethos of ultramannered tennis played in classic whites, Tiger Woods has gracefully diminished the conservative country-club racial hegemony of golf.

A second event—less known, but similar in spirit to the Tiger Woods phenomenon—was the introduction of "Subpar" golfing attire by a design venture-capital firm called Astro Products. Subpar serves to represent the numerous companies bringing new energy to the game, an energy aided and abetted on the cultural front by the release of Adam Sandler's movie, *Happy Gilmore*, and on the technical front by the introduction of exotic materials such as titanium and aggressive new club forms such as the famed Big Bertha.

Such events have not only given golf front-page, center-screen visibility, but they have also challenged the very spirit of the game. Suddenly, golf is a sport of the people, by the people, and for the people. Players of all creeds are flocking to the links. Long-held convictions about the sanctity of golf have been steamrollered by a rock-and-rollified, rapified, and reggaeified panoply of changes. Golf is now a mix of staunch gentility and "alternative" fluidity. The new golfers—already given to a slacker-type freestyling approach to life—have raided the time machine to construct a new identity for the sport that is part fifties suburban dad, part sixties muscle car mechanic, part seventies nerd, and part eighties successful capitalist dude. To quote the Beastie Boys—which Subpar does on its promotional postcards—"It's the *new* style." Subpar is but one example of the new alternative energy finding expression in golf. And if this kind of sea change, this new-found fluidity of identity can happen in and around golf, then it can happen anywhere.

Skate or Die: "Boredom is a Crime"

In contrast to golf, skateboarding has been on the radical fringe from the start; it has always been a renegade activity and probably always will be. With passionately dedicated participants and an indelible cool factor, its cultural premise exists in opposition to whatever the consensus happens to be. It has rejected most attempts at commercialization, and its most ardent adherents never quite fit in—and

Kryptonics Skateboard Wheels
Courtesy Kryptonics

TOP LEFT: **Retro K.** Classic surf graphics have been applied to the Kryptonics Retro K.
TOP RIGHT: **Classic K.** The Classic K replicates the original skateboard wheel designed for slalom and long-board skating, updated with supercompliant, high-rebound, and long-wearing urethane.
LEFT: **Kryptonics Hawaii 5K**. This wheel is designed especially for longboard cruising.

RIGHT: **Nuwood Skateboard (1995).** Traditionally, skateboards are constructed with the wood of North American sugar maple trees. According to designer Tim Piumarta of Santa Cruz Skateboards, the objective of the Nuwood board was to "replicate the cellular structure of solid wood." The one-part, mold-injected, carbon fiber board has the density of wood, but is more durable, more resistant to moisture, and more slippery; it is also recyclable. Courtesy Santa Cruz Skateboards

they work hard not to. Their graphic look and equipment design highlights this "outsider" attitude of willful disobedience.

At the turn of the century, architect Adolf Loos stated "ornament is crime," but in late-twentieth-century, skate-centric culture, it's more like "boredom is a crime." Even the undersides of the boards have become elements of the design equation, as have the wheels, which are differentiated by color, pattern, and material to address a range of riding styles and surface conditions. The killer graphics of boards range from the early surf-inspired Rat-Fink (giant head, little legs, bugged-out eyes) to seventies Retro (when urethane wheels were developed to revitalize the sport) to crazy-haired Street Punk (with its "Skate and destroy the fear" ethos and comic book-style raunchiness) to nineties digital age imagery.

Beyond such graphics, though, the coolest thing about skateboarding is its open invitation to skaters to custom assemble components into a no-fuss, no-muss, totally individualized product. It's as if a consumer who wanted a car could specify parts from the optimal chassis, transmission, and engine to specific seats, paint job, and upholstery. Users get exactly the product they want, assembled on site to order. Boards are further customized through use—abrasions, calligraphy, graffiti, decals, and other assorted forms of advanced user-induced scarring. Skate-boarders take their boards through a process of "post-market product alteration" whereby the existing, mass-produced object is personalized, over time, until it has exactly the qualities and personal fit that the owner desires.

Stephen Peart of Vent Design Associates notes that a skateboard first communicates an image—and then develops that image into a personality through use. He suggests the relationship between a skateboarder and his board is similar to that of a musician and his instrument: intimate, trusting, mutually supportive, and about doing everything together.[2] Peart used this analysis—along with injection-molded, recycled nylon combined with carbon fiber in a microcellular matrix—to create the Nuwood skateboard for the industry-leading Santa Cruz company. The board is a perfect example of what the new generation of sports equipment represents: emotional commitment by the user that is then reflected back into the visual intensity of the equipment as it is envisioned by the designer.

As it has also enriched other board sports, skateboarding has been newly energized by their emergence. Historically, it seems to have mainly evolved out of surfing, as a way for the surfer to practice being smooth on the board. Today, however, skateboarding and street luging have taken skate consciousness in new directions, while snowboarding has emerged from both surfing and skating cultures and supports its own state-of-the-art board graphics. Snowboard graphics, particularly those by such companies as Burton, Option, Alien Workshop, and K2 are more subtle, wittier, and more beautiful than any other boards from other sports—with the possible exception of certain classic skateboards.

Since the late eighties, many of the K2 snowboards have emerged from the team at Modern Dog Design, Robynne Raye and Vito Costarella, who see

RIGHT: **Street Luge Board (1995).** Street luge looks for its origins to the unlikely intersection of traditional alpine sledding and the street culture of skateboarding. Essentially, however, skateboarders have always laid down on their boards, and the advent of a new sport was but a hill away. Recent boards, such as this one designed by Shawn Goulart, have been pared down for aerodynamics and have a shorter wheel base. Courtesy Chris Carnel

FACING PAGE: **Modern Dog Snowboard Graphics for K2 (1997).** Offbeat, edgy humor marks the graphics of snowboards emerging from the Seattle studios of Modern Dog. Graphics for K2's 1997–98 snowboards demonstrate the broad range of imagery used today. Courtesy Modern Dog

LEFT: An ad for an illuminated snowboard takes its cues from Crackerjack prizes.

RIGHT (FROM TOP TO BOTTOM): The rainbow of colors and seven rings look to snowboarder Morgan LaFonte's convictions about alternative healing. The rings refer to Chakras—"energy centers"—and the colors to "energy vortexes" visualized during illness.

A sequence of dramatic landscapes and spacescapes were collaged together for the Marcus Hurme pro model.

Dozens of radiating and rotating patterns were distilled into the single center image for the Juju board. A combination of pods and freestyle paintstrokes for the Zeppelin.

Oversized swooping shapes provide appropriate imagery for the Ginzu, a board designed for carving.

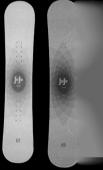

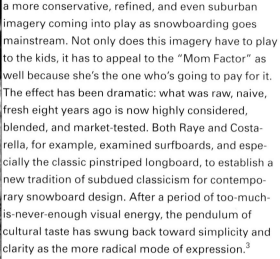

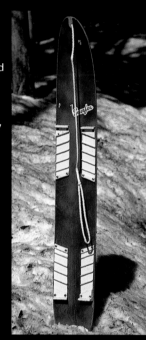

a more conservative, refined, and even suburban imagery coming into play as snowboarding goes mainstream. Not only does this imagery have to play to the kids, it has to appeal to the "Mom Factor" as well because she's the one who's going to pay for it. The effect has been dramatic: what was raw, naive, fresh eight years ago is now highly considered, blended, and market-tested. Both Raye and Costa-rella, for example, examined surfboards, and espe-cially the classic pinstriped longboard, to establish a new tradition of subdued classicism for contempo-rary snowboard design. After a period of too-much-is-never-enough visual energy, the pendulum of cultural taste has swung back toward simplicity and clarity as the more radical mode of expression.[3]

Windsurfing equipment has taken its particu-larly compelling need for a highly refined and adjustable person/product interface and optimized it so that the body itself is used to trim the sail, sup-port the mast, and steer. And surfing, in many ways the inspiration for all board sports, has been re-energized by a new breed of surfers who skate as well as snowboard, and who have brought an "extreme" attitude—along with aerial abilities—to the sport. Surfing today is in a particularly hybridized state; short, "aggro" or aggressive boards and traditional cruising longboards coexist uneasily; in extreme surfing, windsurfers or jet skiers tow surfers into enormous waves where a misstep can lead to paralysis or death.

A measure of air, exposure, and new degrees of "trick freedom" have been transferred from the sidewalk to the waves and slopes; carving has become hypercarving, whether the carving is on the wettest wave or the driest snow. Skateboarders bring their vertical play to the waves, while surfers, always more nature-bound, suggest moves that are more organically connected to the wave. These

athletes, and the cultures they represent, beg, borrow, and steal from one another in an exchange that is every bit as fluid as their physical maneuvers and the medium they perform on. Skate tricks such as those by Christian Fletcher seem even more radical when they are done on water and speak to the easy fluidity of style and action now possible.

Just as skateboarders moved out of parks and pools and started railsliding around town, in plazas, and taking over streets, so have snowboarders eliminated their boundaries. What began with "snurfing" in the seventies evolved into an uneasy coexistence with skiers in the mid-eighties. And just as with surfing and skateboarding, a contingent of extreme snowboarders are now pushing the limits of cross-pollination even further; some surfers now put straps on their boards, just as snowboarders have long done.

Just as skateboarding reinvented, reconfigured, and otherwise reimagined surfing, in-line skating did the same for rollerskating. Before Rollerblade pioneered in-line skating in the eighties, frollerskates (named for the company that created them, frogdesign) reconsidered the rollerskate in the late seventies and used injection molding to replace the leather uppers; with it came brightly colored plastic componentry that was an instant hit. In-line skates built on this precedent and crystallized the fusion of fashion and function that today typifies athletic gear of all kinds. Anyone who thinks such equipment is

K2 In-Line Skaters. In-line skating epitomizes the fusion of fashion and function that is typical of most contemporary sports. Courtesy K2

all show and no go should see the in-line races held at the legendary Laguna Seca auto circuit. As one observer aptly remarked, "If the Futurists were alive today, this is what they'd be doing."

In the nineties, board sports have been merging, cross-referencing, and playing off of one another in both their specific details and in their general culture. Design has become a fluid medium of exchange, a process of communication between the different board factions, a way in which color, pattern, form, and detail can be used to signify allegiances and wordless understandings about what's hip and what isn't. Whether through tech-driven maneuvers or organic freestyling, board sports give the pain of youth a tangible, physical, and aesthetic release. The irony lies in the fact that while these board sports started out being all about doing your own thing on homemade rigs and hand-built gear, today there is an effort to locate a collective soul amidst successes greater than the pioneers ever imagined. Even as an alternative sport like mountain biking now has an Olympic venue, "anti-heroes" ranging from Tony Hawk to Barrett Christy are beginning to challenge mainstream celebrity athletes as voices for youth culture because they seem to be about pure passion, not unmitigated greed.

Shawn Goulart, Street Luge Champion. The leather body suit worn by street lugers is similar to those worn by motorcycle racers. Courtesy Chris Carnel

Innovations and Customization
Come from Passion

At the same time that these voices are changing, so too are the designers. Big ideas don't necessarily come from well-funded research labs, elite committees, or even the biggest brains; they come from the most passionate and iterative processes of experimentation carried out by a group or team of supportive (yet competitive) people who do it because they care and because it's cool, at least to them. Many of today's most influential products have emerged from just such modest origins, a tribute to the interwoven spirits of invention, optimism, and relentless tinkering.

Consider that Op (Ocean Pacific) started when surfers Jim Jenks and Chuck Buttner couldn't find any sturdy trunks. So they cut up one of mom's hefty tablecloths and restitched it into swimwear. Their company brought in hundreds of millions in sales per year in its prime. Likewise, Bill Bowerman used his family's waffle iron to make a prototype for a rubber sole with improved traction, later to be Nike's waffle sole. And outdoor equipment designer Bill Moss used fiberglass when it was still an untested material in the fifties to make stronger, lighter tent poles. The high-strength, precurved aluminum tubing also used by Moss was a product of the aircraft industry, and it reconfirmed to the design community the value of the aerospace engineering tenet to do more with less. The tendency to replace mass with information appears as well in boat design. Brute functionality is being streamlined by computer modeling and high-tech materials. Canoes have gone from wood-strip construction to aluminum sheets to fiberglass strips to cast resins and plastics; the result is an unprecedented lightness, strength, and rigidity.

The great intellectual burst this provides is the realization that there is nothing in nature—and potentially nothing in any successful design—that is extraneous. Good design in sports equipment means that everything matters; every part serves a purpose; nothing is wasted. Such design offers the lessons of ecology—about mutual sustainability, about the value of interconnectedness, and about the place of appropriateness. Efficient design is an especially loaded phrase for those who carry their equipment, as climbers and backpackers do. While there has been a trend toward lighter products—the bike racer, for example, who shaves grams off his or her bike by upgrading components and even drilling parts of them out—the concurrent trend puts high value on adjustablity and physical and psychological acceptability, even if it means greater cost and weight.

Efficiency—and sometimes simply the look of efficiency—has lead to carbon fiber and titanium parts for products ranging from bicycles to camping equipment. Such component shopping allows consumers a new level of customization. Even if it doesn't show a measurable benefit, companies such as Mizuno now offer players of all levels the chance to get a custom, just-like-the-pros-use baseball glove, with the consumer's name embroidered along the thumb. This trend toward personalized sports products is consistent with the larger, societal trend toward customization—witness individualized news over the Internet, personalized desktop software, and have-it-your-way hamburgers, all of which represent the contemporary consumer-choice phenomenon.

It's not hard to imagine that a new type of boutique specializing in sports product change-overs, upgrades, and technical patch kits will emerge. You still may not be able to have your sneakers repaired (a pet peeve of mine—sneakers are almost always thrown out when their weakest link wears out, even though the majority of the shoe is still wearable), but in the future, stores may be more like restaurants where personalized products can be ordered, prepared, and quickly served to satisfy the appetite of the hungry-for-customized-novelty consumer. Have-it-your-way sports equipment orders will soon be the norm.

Learning from Bicycles: How Good Can the Design of Sports Equipment Get?

Bicycles balance the stringent demands for refined aesthetic excellence with the different but even more stringent demands of functional interaction. Advances in design have shifted the paradigm from the rigid, double-triangle metal-tube frame to something more organic, flexible, and open to innovation. In the last ten years, ideas that were considered classic and immutable to change have been swept away by a tidal wave of technologies that include electronic shifting, clipless pedals, aero-componentry, front and rear shock absorbers, monocoque construction, and new frame geometries, along with the use of titanium, beryllium, fiber composites, and metal matrices.

〈ボールパーク〉エアフィット　レッド

イエロー

Mizuno Airfit Baseball Glove (1993). A tube in Mizuno's Airfit mitt can be inflated or deflated with a built-in pump, molding the glove to the size and shape of a player's hand. Courtesy Mizuno USA

Big ideas don't necessarily come from well-funded research labs, elite committees, or even the biggest brains; they come from the most passionate and iterative processes of experimentation carried out by a group or team of supportive (yet competitive) people who do it because they care and because it's cool....

These advances, along with the emergence of a highly competitive new generation of riders, has transformed the bicycle business. In so doing, it has elevated bicycles for many to the status of sacred object. Bicycles have become lighter, stronger, smarter, replacing mass with IQ in a way that goes beyond even what has been accomplished in boat design; physical materiality has given way to higher intelligence componentry. In short, brains have been winning over brawn.

High-performance bicycles achieve what author and essayist Owen Edwards calls "quintessence," in a book of the same name, a kind of radical purity of form and essential clarity of function where nothing can be added or subtracted without losing harmonious balance.[4] By demonstrating a more intimate partnership between user and machine, bicycles now epitomize what well thought-out product design aspires to. Such products tend to offer feedback and encourage customization. They make it easy to make them our own. We attach ourselves to them and foster these attachments for years because they focus our energies in a powerful way. Objects such as this suggest the center *can* hold, contrary to the claims of W. B. Yeats; they suggest that the design of experiences *around* a product are as important, or more important, than the design of the product itself. Most of all, they suggest that optimism may be the most important product designers can create; and that the single most convincing explanation for the success of sports products may lie in designers' abilities to imbue said athletic artifacts with a powerfully transformative sense of possibility.

The social critic Ivan Illich once remarked that an equitable world would conform to the scale of a bicycle, a view that presents the bicycle as a matrix for deciding what shape the world is in.[5] The bicycle, particularly those driven by the demands of sport, is part sculpture-in-motion, part tricked-out life-style machine, and part multipurpose omen for our future—the best symbol yet of our hope for a whirring, nonpolluting, and technologically beneficent age.

Performance as Image/Image as Performance
We live during a transcendent moment in the history of our culture's visual expression. Our sports products are so powerfully designed that they practically create their own sensory overload, but without the accompanying disorientation. Sports equipment—simply in appearance—is a performance enhancer, a kind of drug that we can psyche ourselves up with.

We accept that we don't want to just play a sport; we want to look as though we've mastered it. Traditional ideas about the discipline of practice have given way to a more lenient notion that it's enough to wear the appropriate style, look, or image of the highly-paid professional. Imagistic prowess and the ability to turn heads and capture the gaze of those around you is as important as pure physical prowess and skills achieved through repetition. As a result, a great deal of effort is put into looking like a spectacle—being spectacular—even on the most mundane plays; the concomitant result is an increase in needless mistakes for the sake of transforming an ordinary play into a memorable one.

This points out the fact that we're confused about how we relate to ourselves and how we want to be seen by others. At times, it seems we want people to see our new glasses more than our eyes; our flashy racket more than our belly; our tennis togs more than our legs. We use our sports products to redirect the vision of others. We want people to know us by our expert mix of athletic poses and possessions. We aspire to the right collection of products—this pair of sunglasses, that pair of sneakers. All of which is part of the general psychology of sports in which it's not just about going out and doing it—it's about having a certain attitude that states, as does Andre Agassi's camera commercial, "image is everything."

Selling athletic images to nonathletes—that is, to most of us—is a way of offering us partial identities that we, as consumers, use to create part of our image of who we are. We use the graphics of sports—in the form of caps, logo-laden clothes, shoes, uniforms, and equipment—to inhabit different personas, though only temporarily before we move on to cross-train in our next athletic costume.

This fluidity of identity—apparent in sports equipment, sports culture, and in our own personas as sometime-athletes—may also be in part due to the propensity of Baby Boomers and Generation-Xers to experiment with meditation, fasting, and mind-altering drugs. Pharmaceuticals have probably done more to subconsciously legitimize notions about the shifting nature of reality than any single movie, book, program, exhibition, or other cultural production. Sports products, then, simply continue to build on this theme of the ongoing melding and morphing of identities.

Part of coming to terms with the performance phenomenon also has to do with understanding sports as warfare. From the spectator's viewpoint, many athletes embody the larger-than-life aspects of a transcendent mythological warrior, thanks in large part to media hype and better living through life at the gym. Historically, of course, sports have *always* been associated with contests and combative exercises—consider Roman gladiators, and the

Sadler Safety Jacket (1994). The safety jacket by Marc Sadler was designed as a piece of high-fashion armor for such varied activities as horseback riding, skiing, and motorcycling. It combines soft padding for the chest area and more resistant, harder padding made from composites for the back, shoulders, and elbows. Courtesy Studio Sadler Design

jousting and fencing of medieval times. Today's star athletes continue those traditions, interpreting them, twisting them, subverting them. Many hardly seem real; they're puffed-up like extraterrestrials or a whole new species of man, in pads and weight-reduced armor for highly designed millennial combat, replete with carefully crafted team crests, logos, patches, hats, and helmets.

The battle is staged everywhere—from pristine ski slopes to the muddy mountain bike trail, from the Grand Prix motorcycle course to the local park's bridle path. Gear such as the multisport safety jacket designed by Marc Sadler demonstrates how a singular, combat-ready solution can address the physical aggressiveness of nearly any activity. With articulated, all-in-one-piece, muscle-like stomach ribbings, protuberant composite elbow and shoulder padding, and a highly integrated, skinlike material like that used in high fashion, this groin-to-neck suit seems to have come from the pages of a super-hero comic book: Its radical look is matched only by its equally radical concern for the wearer's physical safety.

Learning from Sports—Where Does It Go From Here?

Designers from all disciplines can learn a great deal from the world of sporting goods. Unexpected juxtapositions of color, texture, and materials occur regularly here. Many products—televisions, computers, and office products, for example—are "boring" in a way that sports products aren't. Teal blue, for example, came in through the NBA via Alexander Julian and the Charlotte Hornets; from Major League Baseball's Florida Marlins; and from the San Jose Sharks of the NHL. Likewise, Nike has incorporated various meshes, molded polyurethanes, elastic fabrics, reground foams, a medley of fastening hardware, and even the incorporation of air itself (the ultimate free, antimaterial) into a series of products unlike any others previously seen.

The energy of these material trends is coupled with—and amplified by—youth-inspired social trends. Among them, the trend to conspire against one's own image; the trend to defy easy interpretation, the trend to willfully and purposefully misinterpret oneself; and the trend to get it wrong just right.

Sports designs that are tapped into such trends enhance life by being in step with where people are going. They embody an anticipatory, idiosyncratic, warped sense of humor; an implied sense of speed and movement; and a biomorphic, organic language that has been super-tweaked to fit the body and given an ironic kick-in-the-ass to match our mental state. Throw in irrepressibility, irreverence, insouciance, and an "I am what I am so accept me" approach to the world, and you begin to get the picture. Embedded in this is a motto for sports design: "Innovate or Die", which was actually the tagline of Specialized Bicycle Components, and was put on their team vehicle—a hearse—in one-foot-high letters before they got their Humvee. Boards, bikes, and sneakers of every type exude exuberance, decisive in-your-faceness, and a relentless abundance of visual calories.

The new millennium's mandate for sports equipment will acknowledge the multiple personalities of users; and it will recognize that the best

FACING PAGE: **Specialized Bicycles**
These bicycles designed by Robert Egger at Specialized are all early form studies and prototypes; while none are in production, all have been tested as future directions for bicycle design. Courtesy Specialized Bicycle Components

TOP LEFT: **427 Cobra Bicycle (1996).** Fashioned after a 1965 Shelby Cobra race car, this theme bike has seven speeds, a banana seat, footbrake, and steering wheel.

TOP RIGHT: **Man-Go Bike (1996).** A bicycle designed for urban transportation, complete with headlights, horn, and removable storage units. The drive train is enclosed in the body so the user stays clean. At once sculptural and functional, it requires little maintenance.

BOTTOM LEFT: **The Suicide Mountain Bike (1995).** Described by its designer as the product of "sex between a mountain bike and a snowboard." Equipped with a "leash" to prevent the bike from continuing down a mountain unattended after a spill.

BOTTOM MIDDLE: **The Harley Davidson Fat Boy Bike (1994).** This bike finds its design origins in the motorcycle. Gas tank, wide handlebars, front suspension, and motor are all, in fact, beside the point—this bike is meant to be pedaled.

BOTTOM RIGHT: **Prehistoric Bike (1993).** Egger designed the Prehistoric Bike to answer the persistent question of who designed the first mountain bike. The wood frame and stone wheels are, in fact, foam, though the sundial positioned on the handlebars is real.

way to reach these users may be through designs that highlight provocation, malleability, and ephemerality. Sports products will become much more personalized, reflecting the desirability of unique solutions and the fluidity of interchangeable information; their emerging international organic language will be based on regional and subcultural design dialects drawn from the visual study of muscles, molecules, movies, fish, nature, and bodies of all types. Such newly conceived sports equipment will articulate a variety of messages; it will increase desire rather than simply meet demand; it will promote stylistic diversity rather than predictable homogeneity; and finally, it will attend to psychological nuance rather than physical fact.

While global current events offer one absurd juxtaposition after the other of our postcredible culture, sports offer a model for embracing the chaos that defines and surrounds us. Given the barrage of information that flows over, around, and through us every day, we don't have the benefit of living in a time of static clarity. But ours is a time of distinct opportunity, and the design of sports equipment is capable of addressing these new benchmarks of complexity, confusion, and contradiction, in the end offering its own new form of clarity. Such a process of integrated yet strategic design points toward a future where sports equipment is created not as a sequence of individual items, but as systems of thought sending either a strongly unified signal or a purposefully fragmented message about the product owner's benefits.

In the future, both players and spectators may have customized screens, projection surfaces, heads-up display glasses, multiple real-time performance measuring displays, and communication-based orthotics of all sorts as part of their playing or spectating gear. Call it the trend to augment and customize our sports realities, to actually feel as if the fan is at one with the athlete. Legions of passionate fans already go to live games with portable radios and televisions so that they can more fully immerse themselves in the entire experience that sporting events have become. Such shifts will increasingly position sports as a creative as well as an athletic profession, and in the process, redefine what sports, marketing, media, and design can do together.

As Tom Wolfe noted when he was writing about the culture of hot rods, these combinations of behaviors, emotions, and ideas produce capital-*A* Art, the kind where money and a slavish devotion to form converge in paradigm-shifting moments of cultural revolution.[6] Sports equipment of all types now offer technological proficiency far in advance of most of our abilities, further raising the stakes for what it ultimately represents. The practical result of this cultish obsession with all manner of things athletic is that the eighties and nineties have been a golden era for sports design in general—and objects such as bicycles, boards, and sneakers have benefited in particular. Just as the fifties and sixties were a penultimate period for appliance and automobile design, our present era's focus on personalized sports and lifestyle products that can empower us, allows us to become more of who we are and who we want to be.

The best sports equipment of today has a transparent quality that is immediately apparent to users and observers alike; its naturalness communicates an integral relationship with the human body and the consumer in no uncertain terms. It fuses the design of motion and emotion with indelible fidelity. It makes for a transparent and tighter interface between person and product, and it has led to shapes that in themselves are three-dimensionally friendly and texturally voluptuous. The realm of design extends from the driving technology behind or inside of state-of-the-art equipment to the entire experience around it.

While it is true that sports teams such as the Dallas Cowboys, New York Yankees, Chicago Bulls, Boston Red Sox, Oakland Raiders, and San Francisco 49ers are idolized by children everywhere, today's youth—the boys, girls, young men and women in the trenches of adolescence who are sweating puberty, inhaling information, and pushing their own mental and physical abilities to the limit on a daily basis—are the real heroes of today. They are the ones enduring and even thriving under the pounding pressures of the past, the crushing challenges of the present, and the impending responsibilities of tomorrow, and the design of sports equipment will always be about their dreams and their realities.

Notes

1. James Gleick, *Chaos: Making a New Science* (New York: Viking, 1987), 8.

2. Stephen Peart, telephone interview with the author, 24 October 1996.

3. Robynne Raye and Vito Costarella, telephone interview with the author, 19 May 1997.

4. Betty Cornfeld and Owen Edwards, *Quintessence: The Quality of Having It and Knowing It When You See It* (New York: Crown, 1983).

5. Rolf Faste, conversation with the author, Stanford University, Palo Alto, CA, 2 February 1991.

6. Tom Wolfe, *The Kandy-Kolored Tangerine-Flake Streamline Baby* (New York: Farrar, Strauss and Giroux, 1965).

Symbol, Status, and Shoes: The Graphics of the World at Our Feet

STEVEN LANGEHOUGH

My Adidas

I like to sport 'em that's why I bought 'em
a sucker tried to steal 'em so I caught 'em
and I fought 'em
then I walked down the street and bop to beat
with Lee on my leg and Adidas on my feet

Now the Adidas I possess for one man is rare
myself homeboy got fifty pair
got blue and black 'cause I likes to chill
and yellow and green when it's time to get ill
got a pair that I wear when I play ball
with a heel inside makes me ten feet tall

my Adidas and me close as can be
we make a mean team my Adidas and me.[1]

THE HIT SINGLE "My Adidas" by the rap group Run DMC underscored the cultural importance that sneakers had attained by 1986. The song helped redefine the role of athletic shoes from standard attire to color coordinated accessory and sign of prestige for which inner-city gang members were willing to rob and kill.

The consumption and display of what we wear confers identity and status. And just as shoes reflect our identity, they can also serve to transform it. Throughout history, the shoe has been viewed as a magical symbol capable of conveying us to a different psychic territory. The Cinderella story is common to many cultures. According to Colin McDowell's *Shoes: Fashion and Fantasy*, one of the earliest recorded versions is a ninth-century Chinese folktale in which a young girl's fortunes are transformed along with her fur slippers. In Charles Perrault's 1697 version of the story, the slippers are made of glass, a material that removes the sexual connotation and more clearly represents her purity and delicate beauty. Bronze and silver shoes have been discovered in the early tombs of Syria and Greece: placing precious shoes with the dead was thought to ensure their travels and fortunes in the afterlife.[2]

In more recent history, the powerful symbolic value of the shoe was spelled out during the 1996 summer Olympics: Nike outfitted runner Michael Johnson with *nine* pairs of gilded shoes, clearly counting on the gold running shoe to serve as a memorable icon for superhuman speed and performance. Johnson proceeded to win two gold medals, obliterating records in the process.

You may not be big enough to play Dominique Wilkins. But you're big enough to wear his shoes.

We've taken Dominique's favorite shoes (size 13), and customized them especially for kids* (boys', size 12½ through 6). So look out big guy.

pump by **Reebok**
IT'S TIME TO PLAY.™

*Adult shoe has a mid-foot and heel bladder system. Because kids' shoe is scaled down considerably, it has mid-foot bladder only.

We can't all play basketball like Michael Jordan or golf like Tiger Woods, but we can go out and buy their shoes. We appropriate the styles of the athletes we admire, clothing ourselves in symbols of what we would like to be, but can't. Shoes are among the most potent of those symbols.

The Pump.™ A mother of an invention.

During the eighties, the unlaced Adidas Classic (BELOW), the Reebok Pump (LEFT), Air Jordans, and the Converse Weapon were fashion favorites. Along with baggy jeans and porkpie hats, these shoes came to stand for hip-hop culture. Professional athletes and rappers became the preferred role models for inner-city male youths, and sport took on an increasing importance in black culture.

The idea of the sneaker as a transforming artifact has been brilliantly marketed by Nike.

Spike Lee and Michael Jordan, both popular black figures with broad appeal crossing over to the white market, appear together in this 1993 television commercial and print ad. Jordan defies gravity with the help of his magic shoes and superhuman work ethic. As he soars overhead, Lee in the persona of the Mars Blackmon character he created for his film *She's Gotta Have It*, tells Jordan, "It's gotta be the shoes....It's gotta be the shoes." Lee's humor plays off Jordan's athletic genius and grace, giving street credence to the myth of "Air" Jordan.

Many inner-city kids see basketball "as a ticket out of the ghetto and become convinced that certain brands of athletic shoes will give them an edge" and help secure their passage.[3] In his book, *Darwin's Athletes*, John Hoberman refers to this phenomenon as the "Black Athletic Aesthetic" and questions its moral legitimacy. According to Hoberman, "sports themes and styles have soaked into the fabric of African-American life, as black identity is athleticized through ubiquitous role models who stimulate wildly unrealistic ambitions in black children—an improbable number of black boys expect to become pro athletes—and imitate athletic fashion trends and hairstyles."[4]

SOMEDAY.

AIR JORDAN. CONDENSED.

Both the athlete and rapper project images that reflect physical power and the aggression of urban street culture. Black feminist Trisha Rose states that rap is "basically the locker room with a beat."[5] Rappers like to compare themselves with athletes; their stage routines require a high level of physical fitness, and many athletes—such as Shaquille O'Neal (OPPOSITE)—also enjoy performing as rap artists. Sport terms are thus appropriated by rappers and given new meanings. The term MVP—meaning "most valuable player" in the rhetoric of sports—denotes "most valuable poet at the mike" in the rap community. This cross-fertilization of terms underscores the role of sports as theatrical cultural events like readings and concerts. Sports have their own choreography and props, sneakers among them.

Not surprisingly, street style has fast become the source for many fashion trends, and shoe manufacturers regularly send designers with their cameras to city basketball courts to document these trends. The Ratball shoe by Adidas (TOP RIGHT), a hot seller among inner-city youth was one product of this field work.

Still, when manufacturers try to acknowledge, and then appropriate, such language and imagery, it can sometimes backfire. It has been reported by Phil Patton that in 1990 Nike sampled ideas for inner-city imagery, naming one brand of shoe "Air Jack." In the language of the street, this can mean "money" or "success"—but it can also mean "kill" or "rob." The name was subsequently changed to "Air Raid." (BOTTOM RIGHT)

WHO SAID MAN WAS NOT MEANT TO FLY.

COME STRONG OR DON'T COME AT ALL.

When there's no such
thing as too short.
Too young. Too old.
Or too strong. You know
you've arrived on Planet Reebok.

"High Flying," a 1993 exhibition at the Institute of Contemporary Art in Philadelphia documented men's basketball shoes as "icons of black identity." Curators Homer Jackson and Lloyd Lawrence observed parallels between basketball, which "glorifies high-flying, quick-thinking athletes," and folktales of a group of seventeenth-century African slaves who created a nation in the Brazilian jungle. The colony defended itself against Portuguese invaders and finally leaped off a cliff to avoid being returned to the bonds of slavery. According to legend, the warriors survived by magically flying back to their homeland.[6]

The curators suggested that modern basketball players have "taken on mythic proportions and that the advertising industry has exploited this image of the black warrior/athlete. Basketball stars and their gear convey a strong sense of power and identity to the black audience."[7] The right pair of sneakers functions as a kind of talisman, instantly conferring athletic prowess. "It's like being able to go to the store to buy a new pouch of magic. You put these things on and you can do just about anything, especially if the sneakers have been ordained by an athlete on TV."[8]

Shoes did not always draw their symbolism from inner-city fashion trends. Indeed, at one time they were more strongly associated with the culture of the suburbs where the most powerful icon was the car. In the fifties, the impact and influence of automobile design was apparent in such domestic appliances as toasters, vacuum cleaners, and irons. The glamour of cars eventually was extended even to shoes: in the early seventies, Converse marketed sneakers with the slogan "Limousines for the feet," a new association at the time.

Today, athletic shoes evoke a fascination with power and style not unlike previous generations' obsessions with cars. If the automobile captured the popular imagination of the fifties, symbolizing the new prosperity of that time, today the athletic shoe has become a more democratic symbol of identity and prestige in multicultural America. Nike shoes, which regularly sell for $150 in the United States, can be sold in Japan for up to $500, and hard-to-find models such as the 95 Air Max have been sold for $1,300. Shoes from the seventies are avidly collected for their antique value and are proudly displayed as trophies in Japanese homes.

Kids hanging out at a Footlocker or Sports Authority can discuss at great length and detail the design features of Air Jordans and Allen Iverson shoes. Phil Knight, founder and CEO of Nike states that "In my era, kids grew up knowing their cars. Kids nowadays grow up knowing their shoes."[9] Andy Mooney, vice president of marketing at Nike, adds that "Today kids know the name and number of every shoe. They know their sku [stock-keeping unit] numbers and prices, just as their fathers knew the names and numbers of every car."[10]

Michael Jordan's love of cars figures into the design of the Air Jordan shoe just as certainly as his skill with the basketball. Nike shoe designer Tinker Hatfield and Jordan meet once a year to design the new model. And just as car design evolves from the top models, "The Jordan" affects the look of more affordable shoes.

> If the automobile captured the popular imagination of the fifties, symbolizing the new prosperity of that time, today the athletic shoe has become a more democratic symbol of identity and prestige in multicultural America.

High performance automobiles were the inspiration for the Air Jordan 8 (RIGHT). According to Nike's promotional literature,

> The shoe was designed to be like a car: the back of the shoe has the look of a suspension system. A cross-pull strapping secures the foot in the shoe, similar to a seat belt's function. The Jumpman logo is like the hood ornament on a Mercedes. The Air Jordan 11 [BELOW] was inspired by convertible automobiles. The contrast from hard to soft, black to white, and from shine to textured on the upper makes it significantly different.[11]

Just as automobile manufacturers introduce new models each season, Nike has release dates for the Jordan shoe. Unlike the car makers, however, Nike keeps the supply deliberately short, allocating top-of-the-line models like the Air Max only to elite shops and in limited supply. Young buyers are aware of release dates and compete to be among the lucky few able to purchase the shoe. Adidas uses a similar strategy, thereby ensuring that demand is self-perpetuating and that shoes remain objects of desire.

WE TOOK THIS IDEA
AND *run* WITH IT.

BLAZER
LIKE A ROCK

Today, the cache of athletic shoes and the popularity of jogging are used to market an array of other products entirely unrelated to footwear. Arthur Andersen, an international financial and business management concern, markets its services with an ad that pictures a running shoe with the accompanying statement: "LONG DISTANCE RUNNERS...HELPING IMPROVE YOUR BUSINESS PERFORMANCE." And even automobiles, the ultimate status symbols of the past, can acquire a desirable mystique through an association with footwear. Honda advertised one sport utility vehicle as its "version of cross-training shoes," while Mercedes projected its high-end logo on the tread of a running shoe.

Limited editions of shoes perpetuate this mystique, ensuring that brand names like Nike and Adidas retain their prestige—what sociologists refer to as "sign value." As French philosopher Jean Baudrillard observes, "Our consumer society is made up of hierarchies of sign values in which one's social status is determined by where one stands within this system of consumption and sign value. Commodities are not the locus of the satisfaction of needs, but confer special meaning and prestige, which serve as indices of social standing in the consumer society."[12]

As recently as 1987 Reebok controlled a third of the athletic shoe market, placing it well ahead of Nike. However, it suffered a loss of sign value, and in 1996 its sales accounted for only 16 percent of the market. Kids may admire the way the Reebok shoe looks or like how it feels on the foot, but they don't buy them because the logo has lost prestige.

Locating trend setters and tracking how the pack follows these trends has become an area of serious study for shoe manufacturers, and this process has been documented by writer Malcolm Gladwell. Reebok sends out "cool hunters" to learn what kids are doing and to test its own design ideas, Gladwell notes. The "cool hunters," for example, gave an Emmitt Smith prototype shoe to members of the Boston College football team. The shoe had a piece of decorative molded rubber on the end of the tongue. When they were returned to Reebok, the molded rubber piece had been cut off. An obvious design change was required; the tongue piece wasn't "cool."[13]

The study of how new ideas and innovations spread is called "diffusion research." According to Gladwell the original ideas are generated from a nucleus of "cool" kids called "innovators" who pick up their ideas from such sources as thrift shops; their ideas of what's "cool" are in large part defined by doing what others are not, or by recombining or

Speed

altering stylistic elements from existing conventions. A respected group observes the "innovators" and they become "early adopters." They, in turn, influence later groups, the "early majority" and "late majority" who would only venture to try what had been sanctioned by "early adopters." Only "innovators," it seems, pay heed to advertising or outside influence in making their decisions—though such advertising messages are frequently twisted, subverted, or otherwise turned on end. All other groups make choices based primarily on peer pressure.[14]

Celebrated professional athletes have been skillfully used by shoe makers to intervene in this "cool" cycle and to influence the fashion choices of "early" and "late majority." Their rebel status in the sports world has conferred a certain coolness on athletes such as Charles Barkley and Andre Agassi— not surprisingly, choices for Nike sponsorship.

Nike's marketing strategy operates on Phil Knight's premise that "in high school, there are only five cool guys who set the social and sartorial standards everyone else follows." Knight reasoned that if he could get his shoes on the most dominant and charismatic runners, the sporting equivalent of "the five cool guys," then the rest might very well come along.[15]

Manufacturers' competition for the next Michael Jordan now begins even before players get to high school. Nike and Adidas vie to have the best inner-city teams wear their gear, cultivating coaches and wooing players at an impressionable age. Players adjust their loyalties and are aware of the fact that the team they are playing for may, in fact, be Nike, Adidas, or Reebok. As one high school coach puts it, "The next time the U.S. goes to war, I'll bet the troops will be wearing Nike helmets."[16]

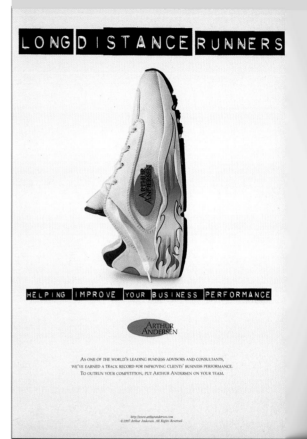

The Van checkerboard slip-on gained instant popularity when Sean Penn sported a pair in the 1982 film *Fast Times at Ridgemont High*. These sturdy vulcanized shoes were first popular with surfers in the sixties and provided an option to the canvas deck shoe. The original Van shoe has evolved from its association with surfers to its present day relation to skateboarders. This transition was effected by the skateboard community, which favored the shoe for its ability to withstand the abuse of toe scraping and heel dragging. The tough, double-stitched upper and bulky sole offered an appealing option to the nylon and foam athletic shoes on the market.

Because of its danger, and in some cases, illegality, skateboarding has been regarded as a renegade sport. Many cities prohibit it on streets where in-line skating and cycling remain legal. The outsider status of skateboarding, with all its disdain for mainstream conventions, has enhanced the appeal of the skate shoe as an alternative to showy, high-tech shoes with gigantic logos and flamboyant graphics. Skateboarders resist the values of popular culture and tend to downplay their gear.

Manufacturers such as Puma, Van, and Airwalk (the latter named after the popular trick of popping the skateboard into the air) have recognized the marketing potential of this subculture and have cleverly used the idea of outsider status in their advertising. Alienation from mainstream values is reinforced through the use of confounding graphics and messages. By featuring extreme sports figures and showing unconventional activities such as rail-bombing and tailgating, some ads go so far as to encourage skateboarders to take dangerous risks.

BEHIND

EVERY GREAT MAN IS

A WOMAN

WHO'S ABOUT

TO PASS HIM.

Women's athletics are taking off. And with it, the sales of Nike women's shoes and apparel. Last year our sales were up nearly 20%. That's because all 369 pieces of apparel and all 171 different styles of shoes are designed not only to improve your customers' appearance, but, more importantly, their performance. Call your Nike representative now. Because women aren't following, they're taking the lead.

In 1994, sales for women's athletic shoes surpassed men's at $5.4 to $5.2 billion. In 1996, U.S. women's Olympic teams brought home gold medals in soccer, basketball, softball, and gymnastics. According to the Women's Sports Foundation, young women's participation in these same sports jumped from one-in-twenty-seven in 1971 to one-in-three in 1994.

The coming of age for women in sports dates to the Nixon era. The 1972 legislation—Title IX—he signed mandated that publicly funded programs offer equal opportunities to men and women, thereby ensuring that all athletes be given access to comparable athletic experiences. Title IX prohibited sex discrimination by any educational institution receiving federal funds, and helped to nurture the pool of talented female athletes at the college and newly forming professional levels. Along with increased participation in sports, Title IX helped to change ideals of beauty and fitness.

The language and graphics of advertising reflect the remarkable change in attitude toward women in sports. By the late seventies, shoe manufacturers had realized that young female basketball players were purchasing men's, rather than women's, basketball shoes. Anxious to meet the growing demands of this new market, they responded with new lines of footwear for women.

Still, their marketing for these shoes reflects a substantial degree of confusion. As recently as 1980, manufacturers were reluctant to use the image of the female athlete to market athletic shoes, believing that women wouldn't respond favorably to images of physical strength or power. An ad from the early eighties selling an aerobics shoe relies instead on an image that is coy, passive, and seductive. If women athletes who were active and in motion were to be represented at all, it was in a traditionally "female" activity such as ballet.

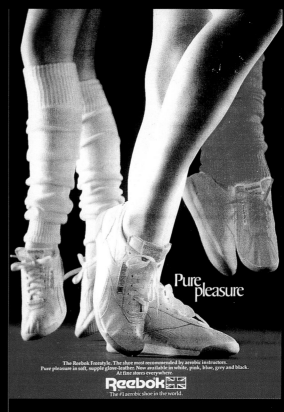

Yes, this is a goddess

but you are not a goddess and you aren't ever going to be a goddess so maybe you should just get used to it. You'll never be perfect *(sorry)* and you're not worshipped *(usually)* and does this matter? No.

Goddesses are worshipped because they aren't real and they aren't us and they aren't allowed to complain. Goddesses are worshipped even though *(and this is important)* they are really stone and really plaster and, more often than not, really dead.

And yes they will never grow old and they will never grow up and they will stay that way *(stay that way stay that way)*. This, however, is not the way you will stay.

Because someday, since you are human, you will notice that time has passed and you are not who you were twenty years ago or ten years ago or even last week. Someday, since you are human, you will notice your body has changed and your face has changed and your kneecaps look more like *(continued)*

Although the company is named after a Greek goddess of victory, it wasn't until Nike recognized the emerging women's market that it put significant financial backing behind women's equipment and advertising. Now, Nike's ad campaigns for women's equipment often manipulate social issues; footwear—and by association, physical fitness—are represented as the implements of women's advancement in society. As writer Michael Lewis observes, "This small transformation in the women's sneaker business is a nice illustration of how in the later stages of social and political change the market leads the way. Put another way, nothing furthers a political cause faster than arriving at a point where there is money to be made off it."[17]

Winston Churchill than ever before.

Do not be alarmed.

Because someday, since you are human, you will decide it is time to take those long walks and run down those streets and push and bend and move your body in ways you'd never thought possible. And it may be harder than you think. And you will get tired and kind of cranky and you may want to stop.

But you won't.

And as you move you will learn to rejoice in your body because it is yours and no one else's. You will learn to rejoice in being imperfect because perfect is such a *complete and utter* bore. You will learn to rejoice in your kneecaps because they are your kneecaps and they have seen the world.

And the goddesses, from some high and chilly mountaintop, will be jealous of you. Let them.

They are stone. You are flesh. They have pedestals. You just kicked the hell out of yours. They can't move. But you can.

Just do it.

For more information about Nike Women's Products, call 1-800-234-2434.

Traditionally, women with muscles were perceived to be threatening; conventional attitudes questioned whether they were "trying to be men." Although such an "image problem," code for homophobic attitudes, still continues to plague some women in sports, current ad campaigns for women's sports deserve credit for helping to dissolve the barriers between beautiful and sexy, athletic and strong. Fashion model and professional volleyball player Gabriella Reese is featured in a Nike ad that presents both personae. The ad projects the attitude that it's okay to be seen as sexy because her athletic ability, strength, and fierce competitiveness have a legitimacy of their own.

Not only do such campaigns promote new athletic ideals, some actually encourage women to step onto the court and compete with men. The blurring of the perception of difference between men and women is apparent in such ads as that stating "basketball is basketball, athletes are athletes." Sheryl Swoopes and two other members of the women's Olympic team challenge men. The narration explains, "This isn't a fairy tale, they didn't beat every guy. But they beat enough to say, basketball is basketball and athletes are athletes."

While such ads break new ground in the representation of the female athlete, both their language and imagery also seem to encourage women to accept some of the worst aspects of men's sports—the violent, in-your-face, taunting culture of men's basketball and football, where sportsmanship has been replaced by trash talking and a general disrespect for one's opponents.

In an effort to address unrealistic portrayals of women in advertising and reporting, the Women's Sports Foundation has issued a list of questions to be considered in reviewing images. Among them: Does the woman look like an athlete? Does she have all of her appropriate clothing on? Is she posed or are her movements realistic? Does the depiction of the sportswoman participating or the theme of the advertisement imply an encouragement or acceptance of unsportsmanlike conduct, lack of respect for opponents, or violence toward other players?

As women athletes continue to take their places at center stage, their image in popular culture will continue to evolve. And while the design of their shoes may signal a new recognition and respect for the woman athlete, the language and graphics used to market these same shoes suggests we still have a long way to go before reaching the finish line of gender equity.

> While the design of…shoes may signal a new recognition and respect for the woman athlete, the language and graphics used to market these same shoes suggests we still have a long way to go before reaching the finish line of gender equity.

if you lose you have no one to blame but me
just do it

gabrielle
reece

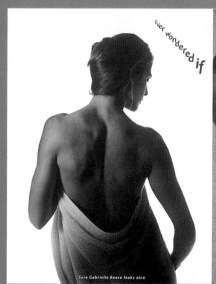

Ever wondered if

Sure Gabrielle Reece looks nice.

looks could kill?

Until you have to play against her.

basketball   is basketball. athletes are athletes.

just do it.

sheryl swoopes

Notes

1. Run DMC, "My Adidas," Protoons Inc./Rush-Groove/ASCAP, 1986.

2. Colin McDowell, *Shoes: Fashion and Fantasy* (New York: Rizzoli, 1989), 61.

3. Cynthia Enloe, "The Globetrotting Sneaker," *Ms.*, March/April 1995, 10.

4. John Hoberman, *Darwin's Athletes* (Boston: Houghton Mifflin, 1997), 4.

5. Quoted in ibid., xix.

6. Homer Jackson and Lloyd Lawrence, "High Flying," exhibition brochure, Institute of Contemporary Art, University of Pennsylvania, Philadelphia, PA, February 13–April 18, 1993, n.p.

7. Ibid.

8. Ibid.

9. Quoted in Randall Lane, "You Are What You Wear," *Forbes*, 14 October 1996, 42.

10. Phil Patton, "Nike Comes Down to Earth," *ID*, March/April 1994, 62.

11. Nike Inc., "Case Studies Draft: Nike Air Jordan Shoes," Beaverton, OR, January 1996.

12. Quoted in Madan Sarup, *Identity, Culture, and the Postmodern World* (Athens, GA: University of Georgia Press, 1996), 108.

13. Malcolm Gladwell, "The Coolhunt," *The New Yorker*, 17 March 1997, 81.

14. Ibid., 82.

15. Kenneth Labich, "A Battle for Hearts, Minds, and Feet: Nike vs. Reebok," *Fortune*, 18 September 1995, 90.

16. Chris Smith, "Sneaker Wars," *New York Magazine*, 3 March 1997, 46.

17. Michael Lewis, "The Capitalist: Just Buy It," *New York Times*, 23 June 1996.

Image Credits

Women: Empowered by the Evolution of Sports Technology

DIANA NYAD AND CANDACE LYLE HOGAN

Nike Lady Waffle Trainer, 1976. Though the first running shoe specifically designed for women was not introduced until 1972, today women buy more running shoes than men. Courtesy Nike Inc.

FROM THE BICYCLES of the 1890s to the highest-tech in-line skates of the 1990s, innovations in sports gear and technology have served as compelling symbols of progress for women. While such developments have meant more speed and strength for men, for women they have represented freedom.

Manufacturers make both more comfortable and more practical apparel and gear for women athletes every year. Introduced in 1977, the jog bra alone provoked a revolution in women's participation in sports and fitness activities. Sporting goods manufacturers now focus a significant part of their research and development resources on the differences between men and women, discerning what women need to perform best and prevent their unique injuries. Scientific laboratories have produced enough studies about the capabilities of women as physical specimens that women, for the first time, see themselves as men do; as natural athletic talents.

The evolution of design and technology in sports science has benefited both genders athletically, but women have been the main beneficiaries from a cultural perspective. For elite athletes—world champions and Olympians—advances in design translate into faster times, gains in power, and easier access to individual potential. For women in general, such advances have a broader reach. They indicate that society is finally acknowledging the female body's full athletic potential instead of just its biological function. It took a long time for manufacturers to respond to the American woman's obvious interest in sports. For example, as of 1972 only one athletic shoe was made specifically for women. Despite the lack of gear designed especially for them, however, female athletic participation skyrocketed during the seventies and eighties, a boom period for women's sports. Finally, by the late 1980s, manufacturers recognized the emergence of women athletes and began producing athletic shoes for girls and women. And in 1996, for the first time, women bought more athletic shoes than men did—148.5 vs. 116.7 million pairs. This demonstration of female purchasing power brought more attention and respect from corporate America than any show of female athletic prowess ever could. The advertising industry's focus on female athletes has recently generated more media attention, which in turn continues to inspire increased female participation in sports.

The Metaphor of Clothing: Liberation

This is not the first time that technological, economic, and media interests have converged to boost public enthusiasm over the female athlete. American sportswomen first emerged in the 1890s, following the first women's rights movement (then referred to in the singular as the "woman's" rights movement) of the mid-nineteenth century. The bicycle became a literal and figurative vehicle for this movement, mobilizing women's entry into a wider field of freedom. The "penny-farthing" came onto the London scene in the latter part of the last century, available to the gentry for leisurely rides around Hyde Park on Sunday afternoons. Women's Victorian garb made riding the bicycle difficult, however, as the seat was high and had to be mounted from a ladder or some other step aid, and the separated positioning of the pedals prevented sidesaddle riding, as was customary for women riding horses. But with the introduction of bloomers (pantaloons invented by women's rights activist Amelia Bloomer in the 1850s), the new Victorian woman could straddle the penny-farthing, immediately gaining a freedom previously unknown to her. When the "safety" bicycle—with rear wheel brakes and pneumatic tires—was invented, Americans caught bicycle mania too.

We can look back now on what transpired following this first upsurge to see that women's ride to freedom on the back of sport and technology has not been a linear story of consistent progress. From the 1890s through the 1920s, the United States witnessed a golden age of women in sports. In the twenties, English Channel swimmer Gertrude Ederle and tennis champion Helen Wills, to name only two, were celebrated as royalty, receiving the adulation granted to film stars of later generations. But as sport became a cultural institution and a vehicle for power and wealth, it was claimed exclusively by men. After the 1930s, sport became thoroughly identified with men and, increasingly, masculinity.

After 1930, women using sports equipment or wearing sleek sports apparel were seen as appropriators of masculine characteristics. Athletic qualities such as desire, will, determination, and courage were not socially acceptable attributes for women. Indeed, the accessories used by sportswomen reflected the degree of confusion and ambiguity that characterized America's perception of female athletes. For example, the first woman to coach an American women's basketball team in international competition, Lucille Kyvallos, grew up as a fine player herself, participating in pickup games on New York streets and playgrounds, playing one-on-one with men. For a first generation Greek-American, however, the prospect of leaving the privacy of her own home with a basketball and walking publicly through her Queens neighborhood carrying a male-identified object for all eyes to see presented a problem during the 1940s. She solved it by camouflaging the ball inside a woven net bag that ordinarily served as a purse for Greek women. Although it's hard to imagine how a basketball might remain concealed within a net bag that took its shape, Kyvallos claims no one ever suspected the contents of the bag because no one expected the conjuncture of a female and sport.

Perhaps the ultimate example of female resourcefulness in the face of unanswered need is the invention of the jog bra. Protection of the breast area was a long unsolved problem for women. In 1977, runner Hinda Miller, frustrated by the lack of comfort and support she experienced in training and competing in her regular bra, created an alternative. Her design source was, ironically, the jock strap, invented in 1874. Miller sewed two jock straps together to form a rudimentary jog bra. In the first year of production, twenty-five thousand were sold. Almost twenty years later, in 1996, approximately 41.6 million jog bras were sold—to the tune of $300 million.

The jog bra was a significant milestone in the evolution of women's "movement" apparel. Yet a comprehensive study of female athletic injuries and common problems undertaken in 1990 by Nike's Advanced Research and Development division discovered that 31 percent of those surveyed still reported breast-related problems. Excessive breast movement causes discomfort, chafing, and outright pain by straining the supporting fascial attachment tissue, known as Cooper's ligaments. Movement between the breast and the bra can also cause soreness and bleeding. Bra straps, fasteners, and underwires produce extreme discomfort over the long haul of an endurance event or intense training sequence. That all of these problems persisted thirteen years after the introduction of the jog bra says something about our cultural reluctance to accept the female athlete.

Within a society in which cultural thought contested the right of the female to own her athletic self, even her ownership of sports equipment remained under constant contention. Before the 1990s, very little sports gear was made specifically for the woman athlete, and almost no advertising targeted her. Perhaps because recognition was such a long time in coming, the care women athletes lavished on their sports equipment often bordered on fetishism. Women rarely received free gear and never expected the state-of-the-art equipment made for men, so every bat, glove, or pair of skates they did acquire was treated as a precious treasure. To this day, Billie Jean King arranges her rackets just

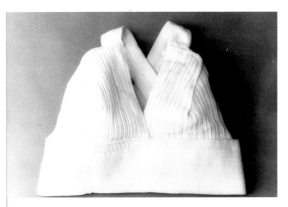

Jog bra (1977). Now a three-million-dollar-a-year retail business, the first jog bra, designed by Hinda Miller and Lisa Lindahl, was made by sewing together two jockstraps. Courtesy Champion

so within her sports bag, laying them out in a particular way at courtside before she begins play. Like crystals used in a ritual of the spirit, women's rackets, goggles, golf balls, softball gloves—not to mention lucky bandannas—all became more than they were because they meant so much. Precluded from owning up in public to their passion to play, many female athletes of not too long ago stroked the accouterments of their secret identities with a lover's passion. (And frequently this usurper of male privilege played that way as well; with a revolutionary's intensity—something still seen today, as the cheering fans of the new professional women's basketball leagues will attest.)

In this context of the past, in which everything associated with sport belonged not just to males, but to maleness itself, our challenge is to imagine not only the courage mustered by women athletes of every generation preceding this one, but also their resourcefulness. Before the 1990s, corporations were not investing their resources—financial

WOMEN: EMPOWERED BY SPORTS TECHNOLOGY

Lycra Shorts (1995). DuPont's high-performance fiber Lycra R Power has been used increasingly for sports apparel. Compression textiles reduce muscle vibration, a factor contributing to muscle fatigue. Courtesy The Rowland Company

shorts and a singlet was born. Today, tight lycra spandex shorts, the newest apparel for female tennis, volleyball, and basketball players, signals greater freedom. Like a second skin that moves smoothly with one's muscles, Spandex gracefully resolves exposure problems.

Not long after English women raised their skirts to ride bicycles, they hemmed them even higher to better chase balls on lawn tennis courts. The dresses worn by women to play both tennis and golf in the late 1800s were so long that they brushed the ground, forcing players to sew a protective strip of leather around the hem. Mary Outerbridge, who introduced tennis to Americans, played in a starched, belted skirt and petticoat, and a high-collared blouse with a necktie, not to mention a constricting corset. Early sportswomen—tennis players, golfers, and cyclists—made the radical move to shorten their skirts to the boot line, their bloomers extending from the hem of the skirt to the ankles. And the elasticized bottom could even be pulled up to allow for more freedom of motion. Movement was always the motivation for lighter materials and less constraining styles. In turn, those materials and styles afforded women even greater freedom of movement. How far freedom of the body could advance women within the body politic could not have been imagined then, but we can see it clearly now—particularly in countries where sexism remains overt.

While the woman athlete is being embraced by American business and technology for the first time, women in many foreign countries are still fighting for equality. Syrian Olympic heptathlete Ghada Shouaa, for example, has become a champion for women's rights in her devoutly Muslim country. Because Muslim religious practice mandates veils and long dresses, her countrywomen

or otherwise—in the design of equipment for women. Individual women, however, often did. In prudish Victorian times, women played tennis in clothes that covered them from ankle to wrist—spectators could actually hear their corsets creaking. But by the 1950s, when Gussie Moran first revealed her lacy short underwear at Wimbledon, women were more focused on winning than in conforming to the taboos of showing too much body. Moran and others took it upon themselves to create their own freedom. Until 1959, women track runners competed in long, one-piece suits called bloomers. But when eventual five-time Olympian Willye White enrolled at Tennessee State University that year, she innovated a new style for better leg lift and mobility. She had worn panty-length shorts as a band majorette, and started wearing them on the track. Soon, her coach talked to a clothing supplier, and the standard track outfit of form-fitting

are often discouraged from participating in sports. Shouaa is coaxing the women of Syria to abandon their hampering gowns in the name of political freedom. She also lends her voice to an international advocacy organization for women, ATLANTA +, which has lobbied the International Olympic Committee to ban from the games those nations using religion to justify forbidding women from playing sports. Shouaa is a maverick; the spandex shorts and nylon singlets she wears to compete represent a need for freedom that is deep and broad; her driving limbs signify more than just literal movement, they express progress itself.

The newest in the tradition of women athletes acting as agents of change is Kenyan marathoner Tegla Loroupe, who recognized that her running ability could translate into new liberties for tribal women in East Africa, particularly in the Pokat tribe of which she is a member. For many such women, tribal life entails genital mutilation, polygamous marriage, restrictions on property rights, and a subservient role in the household.

As a young girl, Loroupe wore an ankle-length cotton skirt while her brothers wore cotton shorts. Loroupe complained to her mother that she could run as fast and as far as the boys, but was constrained by the skirt. Her mother's reply was that wearing such a skirt was tradition and she couldn't think of approaching the chief to ask for a change in custom for her daughter. Loroupe then took it upon herself to wear a pair of her brother's shorts and, sure enough, ran ahead of the village boys. As punishment, she was whipped with tree branches until the backs of her legs bled. But she wore the shorts again the next day and again ran ahead of the boys. Whipped repeatedly, she ran in shorts day after day, until the chief finally relented and gave her outright permission to wear the shorts.[1]

Tegla Loroupe. After winning the 1994 New York City Marathon, Loroupe returned to her native Kenya. Photographed with her family and tribal chief, she wears a feather given to her by her mother. A sign of the warrior, the donning of a feather is traditionally an accolade reserved for men, though there was no dispute over Loroupe's wearing of it. Courtesy Ann Roberts

Tegla Loroupe won her first international race, the New York City Marathon, in 1993, barefoot and in shorts. Presented with the keys to a Mercedes-Benz sedan at the finish line, she politely nodded thank you. A week later, back in Kenya, the chief of her village gave her sixteen cattle and nine sheep—an extraordinary gift for a Pokat woman—and she wept with pride. Loroupe has successfully refused the female genital mutilation tradition of her tribe and champions first-ever rights for women throughout Kenya, where polygamy is rapidly losing ground to monogamy. And young girls in tribes throughout East Africa now have the option of wearing shorts instead of long skirts.

While relatively progressive compared to many nations, the United States has nevertheless responded slowly to the needs of the female athlete. Almost nothing was designed specifically for the woman athlete before the seventies. For example, women were competing in marathon running by the sixties, but it wasn't until 1972 that Nike produced its first women's running shoe. Subsequent attempts at improvement were limited, despite the fact that the numbers of female runners were growing rapidly. As recounted in a 1991 book on the history of Nike, *Swoosh*, that company's refusal to take the women's market seriously was a huge blunder that let Reebok stake an enormous claim with its aerobics shoe designed exclusively for women. Nike did not want to risk its "masculinist" image by addressing women's needs.[2] Today, however, over 50 percent of Nike's running market is accounted for by women, so the company's sophisticated team of exercise physiologists and experts in biomechanics study the specific problems of a woman's foot.

At the Nike "campus" in Beaverton, Oregon, Dr. Darcy Winslow, the company's Head of Advanced Research and Development, tests elite women runners on a force platform, a stationary plate that responds to the dynamically shifting forces of foot contact. Individual layers of quartz within the plate generate an electric current when stressed horizontally or vertically. The plate can be embedded in a floor or running track to measure the forces of a sprinter crossing it. Winslow's team has concluded that because women have wider hips than men, they also have a large quadriceps angle, which the team calls the "Q angle." This large Q angle is thought to cause lateral tracking of the patella (the knee cap) and thus renders women runners predisposed to knee problems, perhaps explaining why women runners seem to develop more stress fractures, chondromalacia patella, and joint injuries than men.[3] Because these injuries are thought to derive largely from anatomical structure, new training techniques will not effectively avoid them. Nike now designs its women's running shoes with a narrower heel, less volume in the instep, a longer toebed and a higher arch. Nike also makes gentler lacing for women's shoes, as studies have shown women's veins are generally closer to the skin than men's.

Likewise at Spalding, Anne Flannery, manager of the women's athletic division, observes, "In the past, women's products were made of comparatively cheap materials, and they were often pink. The *p* word we're looking for now is not pink; it's performance."

If young women athletes used to look up to Chris Evert as the icon of a dignified and ladylike winner, they now idolize the highly muscled Teresa Weatherspoon, New York Liberty basketball star, or Missy Giove, the top

> At Spalding, Anne Flannery, manager of the women's athletic division, observes, "In the past, women's products were made of comparatively cheap materials, and they were often pink. The *p* word we're looking for now is not pink; it's performance."

Missy Giove, 1997. With body piercing and a punk coif, extreme cyclist Missy Giove has radically revised images of the woman athlete. Courtesy Bliss Images and Cannondale Bicycle Corporation

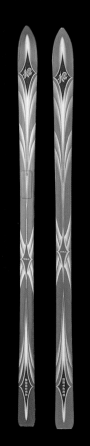

Women's Sport Bike Saddle (1996). The nose area at the base of this women's bike saddle designed by Georgena Terry has a cut-out to relieve pressure and allow for ventilation. Courtesy Terry Precision

K2 Women's Skis (1996). Sidecut skis have been redesigned by Anthony DeRocco of K2 to address the needs of women alpine skiers. Because a woman's center of gravity is shifted slightly back from a man's, the mounting point—the placement of the binding—has been moved forward. A different mix of fir and spruce is specified for a lighter, more flexible ski. Courtesy K2

professional mountain biker in America. Giove races down mountains at 60 miles-per-hour, rides a custom-made, fire-engine red bike with enormous shock absorbers, has broken thirty bones racing, and wears her dead pet piranha and the ashes of her childhood dog in a sack around her neck. Giove's musical tastes run toward Rage Against the Machine—and she likes the volume loud. Every movement she makes, on or off her bike, screams "Out of my way! Individual coming through!"

How many nonathletic high school girls wear the baggy clothes of Missy Giove's extreme sports youth culture, making their own declarations of individualism? How many urban women walk to the office in sneakers, only to switch to the obligatory pumps once upstairs? Many of the fashions and habits of today's women originated in the sports world. This has been true of men for a long time, but for women it is a relatively new phenomenon. The demand for women's products did not become strong until the mid-1970s, after Title IX federal legislation opened the school arena to female athletes. And it has taken twenty more years for the corporate economy to respond.

High-Tech Gear: Just For Women

Innovation in apparel for women athletes is being followed quickly by the similar introduction of a variety of athletic and recreational gear designed specifically for the female physique. It's not just fashion. Manufacturers' brochures promote bicycle saddles with softer noses to prevent vulvovaginal injuries; alpine skis that are weight distributed for a woman's lower center of gravity; climbing harnesses with narrower cinches; boxing chest protectors; backpacks with narrower widths; and sleeping bags with wider hip areas and double insulation at the feet (women's extremities don't adapt to cold as well as men's). One of the leading outdoor gear manufacturers in the United States, The North Face, takes the women's market seriously enough to hire female athletes to test its products. Lisa Gnade, a top competitive rock climber, advised the company last year to design "a backpack with several compartments so that ropes and shoes aren't mingled with clean clothes.... Who wants to put on a down vest that's caked with filth after climbing all day?"[4]

K2, of Vashon Island, Washington, set a precedent in 1986 by developing the first skis specifically for women. These models were designed with lighter materials and a softer flex pattern to accommodate a woman's lower center of mass and reduced body weight. K2 has also been an innovator in the design of in-line skating equipment for women. Of the twenty-four million in-line skaters in the United States today, half are women. But until three years ago, no skates were designed specifically for female feet. Skates were plastic shells, like ski boots, with moveable inner linings, and women simply used a man's boot with a bigger lining. In 1994, K2 created "softboot" technology for in-line skates, a design that addresses women's physiology and biomechanics. For instance, because of their proportionally larger Q angle, women, when using typical hard-shell skates, are often forced to skate on the inside edges of their wheels. With K2's women's models, however, the frame and base are aligned so that the toe points slightly inward. This allows the skater to keep off the inside edge by centering her weight more directly over the skate chassis. K2's women's skates are also specifically designed for narrower heels, higher insteps, and wider toes. Because the leg muscle mass is located lower in the calf in females than in males, K2's most recent innovation is a lower cuff, cut in the shape of a V, to accommodate that mass.

K2 In-Line Skates for Women (1996). K2's tongue-in-cheek marketing for women's products demythologizes the brawn of the male athlete by asking whether traditional men's in-line skates "drink too much and pick fights with other skates?" Courtesy K2

Amy Buckalter, Vice President and General Manager of K2, North America, claims that progress for women has been a chicken-or-the-egg process: women are participating more than ever in fitness, recreation, and sports activities, motivating corporate America to cash in on a huge and expanding market by catering to their needs. Conversely, women are participating in bigger numbers because there is finally gear actually made for them; gear that fits the female anatomy, takes the

Spalding Woman's Softball Glove (1994).
A Neoprene innerglove system allows this mitt to be customized to fit women's smaller hands without compromising the standard exterior dimensions of the glove. The new design also realigns flex points and palm padding, both of which make it easier to close. Courtesy Spalding Sports Worldwide

While skates and other sorts of gear that acknowledge women's needs are available, bicycles designed for women remain difficult to find. Georgena Terry, 5 feet 3 inches tall and an avid cyclist, recognized a decade ago that she and her female friends could not find a bike to fit them properly. Terry put her education in mechanical engineering to the task and designed a new configuration to match a woman's shorter reach. One female mountain bike tester returned from a ride on one of Terry's bikes to say: "When I got home after a two-hour ride with no cramps in my shoulders, I realized that it was because I'm used to being stretched too far over my own bike—which is, yes, a man's model."[6]

In golf, efforts to accommodate women have been more cosmetic than conscientious. Joan Joyce, arguably the greatest fastpitch softball hurler of all time and a player on the Ladies Professional Golf Association tour for over a decade, speaks bluntly of the equipment available in the fifties, sixties, and seventies. "Golf clubs for women were just horrible." The only option to get proper fitting clubs was to pay handsomely to have them custom made. Even now few pro shops have recognized the emergence of the power-hitting, competitive female golfer. Fed up with "male pros who seem to think that women want to look like ten-year-olds, with lace and bows on their bags and pink-and-blue shafts that look like toys," in 1993 Patricia Dixon opened a Dallas shop called "Empowered Women's Golf." Now the leader in full-service pro shops just for women, it has expanded to fifteen stores.

Women tennis players, both professional and recreational, have been beneficiaries of the evolving technology in lightweight rackets. In the professional world, the wood racket had disappeared by

female's biomechanics into account, and addresses female attitudes about sports.[5] Buckalter is a rare instance of a female brand manager at an in-line skating company, but in her two years at K2 she has witnessed the hiring of women as engineers for product development and as marketers for corporate strategy. Women at Nike, Reebok, K2, Spalding, and elsewhere are having an impact, proving that there is an enormous profit center with women's products, and that profit center is creating authentic, high quality, performance-oriented gear specifically for women.

the early seventies, after injuries from the heavy wood had affected women competing on an expanding schedule of tournaments. In 1974, the first oversized racket, the Howard Head Prince Classic, offered a 50 percent increase in hitting area. Developments that allowed players to achieve more and more power quickly followed. Aluminum, steel, and graphite composite materials made for lighter rackets. Whereas the old wood rackets weighed 13 ounces or more, today's graphite versions weigh roughly 9 ounces. Along with lighter weight, these stiffer rackets also offer more power, augmented further by the redistribution of weight toward the head of the racket.

The technology aimed at the power game has adversely affected the spectator appeal of men's professional tennis. Strong servers such as Goran Ivanisovich may win entire matches on aces without having to play out points or include finesse in their repertoire. Women, on the other hand, are applauded for their improvement in power. Players such as Brenda Schultz McCarthy wield deadly serves, and new serve-and-volley players, such as phenom Venus Williams, have dazzled opponents and spectators alike with their powerful strokes.

Po-Jen Cheng, a chemical engineer and racket designer at Wilson, says all of that company's innovations are now geared toward women. Their mission is to enable women players of all levels to hit the ball with more velocity and less strain on their joints. This is a far cry from the company's position twenty years ago, when it produced only a single racket for women, the signature Billie Jean King. When thousands flocked to stores to buy the racket after King beat Bobby Riggs in the 1973 "Battle of the Sexes," the company's stock was quickly depleted.

The emergence of the woman athlete during the 1970s catalyzed the first American fitness move-

Lady Cobra II and Lady Cobra II Offset Golf Clubs (1996). These clubs have lighter shafts, grips, and heads designed for female golfers. Additionally, the shaft flexes at a lower point than on a standard club in order to compensate for women's slightly lesser swing speeds. That the equipment is marketed as "ladies' " rather than "women's" equipment reflects the conservative culture that persists in golf. Courtesy Cobra Golf Incorporated

ment on a large scale, as huge numbers of men and women began running. A generation later, women still comprise the majority of new participants in fitness and recreational sports. The 1996 Sporting Goods Manufacturers Association (SGMA) annual survey reported that the stationary bike, the most popular piece of fitness equipment in the United States since 1987, had been replaced in popularity by weights. According to Gregg Hartley, executive director of the Fitness Products Council, weight training among women is responsible for the new trend. In the survey, the number of females who reported working out with weights at least once per week increased 77 percent from 1987 to 1996. Hartley makes a direct connection between women overcoming a previous reluctance to lift weights and the new development of equipment made just for women. Smaller, narrower machines recognize a woman's frame. And more machines are now geared to work the hips and thighs, areas of concern for women.

The proliferation of home gyms also highlights the popularity of weight lifting among women. According to the SGMA, the second fastest growing sport for women in America is working out on a multipurpose home gym. Treadmills, stationary bicycles, step machines, cross-country skiers, abdominal crunchers, and free weights are all products that women are investing in for their homes.

Machines: The Last Male Bastions or the Ultimate Equalizers?

Insofar as males in Western culture traditionally have received more education in mathematics, engineering, and physics than women have, it is understandable that men still hold most of the jobs as designers and testers of technology in sports. But when it comes to participating in sports and recreational activities in which machines are the key to performance, gender need not be a factor. In equestrian sports, athletes often give credit to their horses, which can thus be seen as equalizers between the genders. Similarly, the car, the plane, the balloon, and the boat are all faster and stronger than any human athlete. Male athletes, then, relinquish advantages of speed and strength when they compete in machines. In aviation, pilots rely instead on quick thinking, judgment, scientific knowledge, and instinctual reaction to the elements; if these are the winning traits of an aviator, then males and females should be able to fly side by side. And they do. The female fighter pilots who flew actual combat missions during the Gulf War were accepted and respected by their fellow male pilots.

We are in the habit, however, of categorizing machines, gadgets, and all things technical as "male." Yet women embraced racing machines from their very beginnings, and, in fact, these machines often used female imagery for marketing purposes. Print ads from the twenties often pictured women flying around a curved country lane in an open-air roadster—hair and scarves blowing wildly in the breeze, cigarette holders clenched in their teeth—as symbols of defiant independence.

At the turn of the century, several accomplished French women made their marks in aviation—long before the famed Amelia Earhart made hers. Blanche Stuart Scott, who, in 1910, became the first woman to drive across the country in a car, became the first woman to fly solo in a plane shortly thereafter. In 1912, seventeen-year-old Harriet Quimby became the first woman to fly solo across the English Channel.

Now that rifles and bows and arrows have evolved from weapons of strength (and symbols of class status) to items of high-tech telemetry, women have entered the sports of shooting and archery in large numbers. Roughly 7.5 million American women actively participate in target shooting, an increase of 80 percent since 1988. Most popular are sporting clays and skeet shooting, but trap shooting, handgun target shooting, and rifle target shooting are frequent choices as well. Canadian Susan Natrass is a thirteen-time National Champion in the single-bore rifle event, competing directly against men. Tammy Forster has won two World Cups in the ten-meter air rifle event. Forster became a master shooter by developing a concentration level that actually allows her to pull the trigger in between heartbeats. She calls the ten-meter air rifle "the most cerebral of sporting events."[7] Annie Oakley told us women were expert shots one hundred years ago, but now technology proves it.

In 1996, an all-women crew competed in the America's Cup yachting races. The success of their boat, America3 ("America Cubed"), brought down another barrier for women the world over. Sailing is considered the oldest modern sport and remains a haven for sexism. Resistance to the female team

America3 (1996). Technology has helped to level not only the playing field but the ocean as well. The all-woman crew of America3 participated in the semifinals of the 1996 America's Cup yachting race. Photographs © Daniel Forster

within the upper-crust sailing community was fierce. Dennis Conner, widely viewed as America's top sailor, evidently threatened by the new competition, resorted to the establishment's last-ditch weapon against sharing the sport with women, and throughout the summer of 1996 made assorted gender derogatory remarks to the press about the women's crews. The costs for Conner's "Stars & Stripes" team in the last America's Cup races in San Diego were about $15 million. The owner of the America3 team, Bill Koch, estimated the cost of his sponsorship at about $60 million.[8] Koch believes that technology (and the money to buy it) makes the difference in twelve-meter yacht racing. After winning the prestigious Cup in 1992 (with America3), Koch said: "Technology is the key to winning in sailing, not strength…55 percent of a syndicate's success at the America's Cup can be attributed to boat speed, 20 percent due to tactics, 20 percent due to crew work and five percent down to sheer luck. Of crew work, only ten percent can be put down to strength, which only accounts for two percent of the total equation."[9]

The press and the sailing community were relentless in their criticism of the female crew, despite their obvious skill. The emphasis the criticism took was that women were simply not strong enough for yachting. In her paper "Gender and the Perception of Masculinity in Professional Sailing," sports sociologist Sara Crawley explored why men who sail defend their sport against female participation. Sailing is a moneyed sport, reaching back to the posh yacht clubs of the mid-1800s and a tradition in which courage is understood to be within the purview of a privileged male gentry. Yet while the wealthy sailors who dominate twelve-meter racing today may cling to that masculine tradition, the fact remains that only one crew position on twelve-meter

yachts requires strength: the job of the "grinder" who rotates the enormous winches that adjust ropes moving thousands of square feet of sail, often in high winds. Crawley points out the irony that a sport that spends hundreds of millions of dollars on technological innovations for every America's Cup competition still relies on manual rather than electronic winches. Her inference is inescapable: that the grinder may most of all be an accessory that keeps notions of male superiority afloat.[10] The factor of strength becomes further moot when we learn that each of the women grinders on the America3 boat could bench-press around 200 pounds, and had no trouble working the winches. In the end, America3 won a number of qualifying races, and was not eliminated until the semifinal round.

Contemporary versions of the "machine as equalizer" concept can be found in the extreme sports practiced by so many members of Generation X: sky surfing from airplanes, luging down streets at 55 miles-per-hour in asbestos suits, mountain biking down icy slopes at 65 miles-per-hour. All of these sports are practiced in relatively "gender-free" environments, suggesting that this newest generation of athletes seems little preoccupied by stale notions of male superiority. It is, of course, an attitude that benefits men as well as women. Many young men are disenfranchised in the limelight world of the "Big Four" power sports (baseball, basketball, football, hockey). Lacking size or muscle bulk or eschewing conventional team sports, they may turn instead to outrageous feats of daring to distinguish themselves and express their physicality. Rather than boasting about the touchdown catch on Friday night, they may instead gain esteem with stories of jumping 20-foot fliers on their snowboards. And though the ratio of males to females participating in extreme sports is about three to one, the sheer numbers involved means that some five million girls and young women are taking risks, too. Most of these extreme events— bungee jumping off high bridges, for example—rely neither on strength nor speed, but depend instead on equipment, preparation, and sheer, daredevil guts. Not surprisingly, such high-tech sports as in-line skating, snowboarding, hang gliding, rock climbing, downhill mountain bike racing and sky surfing are attractive to the female faction of Generation X.

In 1996, the fastest growing sport for women in America, based on frequency of participation, was in-line skating. As previously noted, the SGMA estimates that half of the total population of in-line skaters are women.[11] While most of those women may be skating for fitness and recreation, claiming that the lack of punishing impact, the freedom of movement, and sociability factors draw them to the sport, a healthy number are simply drawn to the thrill of "grinding the rails"—that is, jumping up onto a handrail, skimming along with an extreme knee bend, then flying off onto the concrete. K2 estimates these radical risktakers compose about 15 percent of its market. And the (gender neutral) ultra-baggy pants, huge T-shirts, and oversized jackets of the snowboarding set are the apparel choices of in-line skating grinders, too.

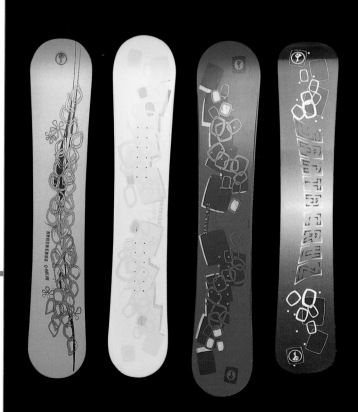

TOP: **Morgan LaFonte.** Professional team rider Morgan LaFonte. Courtesy K2

BOTTOM: **Santa Cruz Q-Type Snowboards.** The width, stance, length, and flex of Santa Cruz's Q-type boards, designed by Shaw Kaake, have been constructed specifically for women. Courtesy Santa Cruz

The Inner Technology: Body Chemistry

At the 1928 Olympics in London, several women collapsed after crossing the finish line of the 800-meter run. Though, it was not unusual for men to faint or fall to the ground exhausted after a run, Olympic officials took advantage of the sight of women gasping for air, dropping the event from the games for over three decades. On the pretext of protecting their childbearing futures, women were prevented from running farther than the equivalent of a city block in the Olympics until 1960. The 1928 incident served the myth of female physical fragility and inferiority well into the seventies, when a series of events came to symbolize a general cultural shift that forever altered the relationship between American women and sports. In 1973, Billie Jean King defeated Bobby Riggs in the aforementioned "Battle of the Sexes," which was televised nationally; four years later, in 1977, Janet Guthrie became the first female driver to compete in the Indianapolis 500; and in 1979 Diana Nyad bettered the men's world record by swimming 102.5 miles from the Bahamas to Florida nonstop, the longest recorded swim in history.

The barrier-breaking exploits of female athletes during the seventies led to objective athletic testing at academic research centers, where women tested not only comparably to men, but actually superior to them in some endurance categories. Their buoyancy, especially in saltwater, made them suited to ocean swimming. Their ease at acclimatization was noted, and women have since become the captains of many ascent teams for both Mt. Everest and K2, the two highest peaks in the world. Other endurance tests—the ability to tolerate high acidity, the efficiency of thermo-regulation, and the use of energy stores, for example—have shown women to be the equals of men in certain physical aspects.

Joan Benoit, who won the gold medal in the first Olympics to offer a women's marathon (Los Angeles, 1984), does not have the appearance of a world-class athlete. Not only is she small, at 5 feet 3 inches and 110 pounds, but she has not developed an impressive, defined musculature. Excellence in marathon running, however, does not come from a carved physique. Signs of superiority lie in the measurement of VO_2, or the amount of oxygen taken in to fuel the muscles during exertion. A world-class male endurance athlete uses about 70 millimeters of oxygen per kilogram of body weight per minute. Joan Benoit, in her prime, used 79, a measurement that in part explains her excellence. When such statistics were published, they gave scientific credibility to what everyone could see with their own eyes: female athletic excellence.

In his 1992 book, *Mortal Engines: The Science of Performance and the Dehumanization of Sport*, John Hoberman analyzes the pitfalls of unlimited technological experimentation in the quest for higher human performance levels. Hoberman divides the world of science into two eras: the first, the age of scientific truth, during which we simply recorded facts once we discovered them, and the second, the age of calibration, during which we became obsessed with modifying our natural limitations. In the latter scenario, modern sport is pure technology.[12] Imagine that we know that the difference between an Olympic gold and silver medal in a track sprint is two hundredths of a second. And imagine that we have made sure that our athlete owns the best spikes available, has perfected the blast out of the blocks, has been analyzed on film to maximize the efficiency of stride and arm action, and is running on the fastest rubberized surface in the world. What is left for us to pursue in our obsession for pushing the edge of the envelope of this athlete's performance? Confidence or focus may be the Zen answer. There is also the complicated realm of endocrinology.

All human movement relies on the use of adenosine triphosphate (ATP). A cellular reaction within this molecule causes muscle contraction. An educated coach knows how to use intervals, fartlek (mixes of speeds without stopping), and other forms of "periodic" training, to develop the most efficient ATP production. And sophisticated athletes know how to keep production of lactic acid, a by-product of metabolizing carbohydrates that inhibits muscle contraction, to a minimum. The body may be infinitely complicated, but most world-class athletes have nonetheless been tested and trained for improvements in body processes such as anaerobic glycolysis, whereby the cells break down carbohydrates to make more ATP.

All of these areas of study could have particular relevance for the female athlete. If we continue to accept the myth that the male is physically superior, then the pursuit to secure the woman athlete's full potential might turn to re-engineering the chemistry of a woman's body. Hoberman concocts a futuristic vision of artificial bodies, and in his book it is women who undergo the most radical metamorphoses.[13] Consider steroids.

Anabolic steroids have been illegally used by some athletes since about 1935, when they were first synthesized as derivatives of the male hormone testosterone. First widely used by Soviet weight lifters for added muscle mass and explosive strength, anabolic steroids came to the West in the fifties and still present a tricky testing problem for the governing bodies of various sports and the International Olympic Committee. Coaches and athletes, always a step ahead of the testers, are adept at disguising the drugs in their systems. Women,

however, have received a double blow from the use of steroids. Not only were they subject to steroids that increase strength, but also they fell prey to coaches and government officials who gave them a different kind of steroid to stave off the onset of puberty; young female gymnasts in Eastern Block countries in the seventies were the most notable victims of such drugs that, secretly administered, kept the pelvic girdle narrow, prevented breasts from developing, and stunted growth of the long bones. The girls thus stayed tiny, their prepubescent bodies better suited for the quick tumbling maneuvers of the sport.

Obviously, experimentation with human chemistry occasions ethical questions. Hoberman raises doubts about the difference between changing one's strength potential with an illegal substance such as a steroid that already exists naturally in the body, and using other artificial, though legal, techniques, such as electric muscle stimulation (EMS).[14] It is not unreasonable to assume that such issues might affect women with special force; the female body has been an object of contention and manipulation throughout history. Is it possible that the biology of a woman's body might be re-orchestrated to mimic that of a man's? Is it possible that women themselves could be convinced that the redesign of their bodies would be empowering?

On a more positive note, we have seen that naturally occurring changes in a woman's body make her a better athlete, without technological or scientific intervention. Ingrid Kristiansen of Norway, silver medalist in the 1984 Olympic marathon, ran the best times of her career after the birth of her first baby. Kristiansen's post-birth performances led to a series of studies of women athletes from different sports. These established that pregnancy seems to improve athletic performance after childbirth, not only in endurance events but in short sprints as well. While there is no empirical data as to how or why a female athlete hits a superior stride after childbirth, anecdotal evidence is mounting. As did Kristiansen, Joan Benoit posted some of her fastest times after childbirth. Basketball star Sheryl Swoopes returned to her WNBA team, the Houston Comets, a short six weeks after the birth of her son—and helped lead the Comets to the playoffs.

Discoveries made in testing women athletes can lead to the improvement of health among the population at large. Women athletes have been the subject of several studies on bone density. By significantly increasing their bone mass with resistance training, athletes have led orthopedists to reconsider ways in which osteoporosis might be staved off in postmenopausal women. Now, most gerontologists and orthopedists recommend weight training for older women as one way to prevent bone density from declining to fragile and debilitating levels.

Scientists aren't the only ones looking more closely at women athletes. The advertising industry is on the watch as well, both reflecting and shaping our views of the modern sportswoman. Current ad copy for women's sports products tells the story of a continued quest for freedom on the part of women. Men are urged to buy rackets, golf balls, and sneakers by ads that tell them they will be able to serve harder, hit farther, and run faster. Women are told a different story: that by buying the advertised products, they will be better human beings, less victimized by their social situations, and freer from their problems.

Avia adds for women state that "You jump, run, lift and dance. Until, finally, your troubles are too tired to keep up with you." Nike goes farther in its use of provocative social issues to market footwear. One recent ad campaign seemed to pose as a public service announcement for the prevention of domestic violence: the photograph of a young girl was accompanied by the words, "If you let me play, I will like myself more, I will have more self-confidence, I will suffer less depression, I will be 60% less likely to get breast cancer, I will be more likely to leave a man who beats me." The complex emotional bartering evident in relationships where abuse is constant and repeated is one of society's most serious issues, and it is difficult to believe footwear can enter the equation as a solution to the problem.

Ads for New Balance footwear suggest that "You can run to become a better runner. Or you can run to become a better mother. Or a better doctor. Or a better teacher. Or a better friend. You can run to become a better runner. Or you can run to become better." New Balance ads for men simply run through the days of the week with different combinations of the words "Father," "Husband," "Banker," "Friend." The difference between the two ads is subtle, but clear: men simply perform these different roles with ease, while women, with all their presumed low self-esteem, exercise out of a mania for self-improvement. Corporate America is responding to the huge surge of female participants in fitness and sports activities by manufacturing more products for women and by designing products specifically for the female anatomy. In doing so, it is meeting genuine needs. Yet many of the images used to market these products seem to rely on familiar, stale clichés that reaffirm patronizing attitudes toward women in sport.

It's no coincidence that the American romance with sports began at a time when we embraced technology and the Industrial Age. The turn of the last century marks the beginning of "modern" sport—with all its mania for measurement and quantification and its associations with higher purpose within the social hierarchy. American ideals of progress were also developing full-throttle, along with notions that a newly unified country could mobilize itself along the lines of scientific, technological discoveries, experimentation, and exploration. Whereas sports had previously been all play and no work (mixed in with some ancient, seasonal rituals), they became tools for a newly industrialized nation on the move. Baseball was the premier sport of the industrial age, and it enjoyed equal popularity with both sexes. The earliest record of a women's professional baseball team is in 1867—a black women's team called the Dolly Vardens. They played out of Philadelphia, wore red calico dresses and used a mush ball of yarn.[15] In the 1890s, women began competing in basketball and baseball in college and in tennis and golf at social clubs.

It was a time when men worried about becoming "effeminate." With office work replacing farm labor, and factory machines available for physical labor, between 1890 and 1920 men experienced a "crisis of masculinity."[16] Newly uprooted and sedentary, where would men get the energy to drive the country into the forefront of this new world? In this *fin de siècle* chaos of change, leaders of cultural thought identified a need for renewal and regeneration in the body politic, a transformation that could begin in the human body. The idea that people might transform themselves through physical movement was new in America. And such transformative powers derived their most vivid manifestation from what was happening to the female body at the

time. From the stereotypical Victorian female—physically fragile, psychologically frail and prone to hysteria—emerged the image of the rosy-cheeked, healthy "Gibson Girl." Simply by hopping on a bicycle for a leisurely tour of the countryside, she gained hardiness and, in the assessment of the popular magazines of the time, lost her moodiness. Thus American culture first realized sport's power to change the body and mind by noticing how it put a blush and a smile on the Victorian lady.

Such sudden vibrancy and prowess gave the sportswoman a temporary celebrity. Eleanora Sears was the best all-around athlete in America in 1910, a household name as a champion in tennis, golf,

Corporate America is responding to the huge surge of female participants in fitness and sports activities by manufacturing more products for women and by designing products specifically for the female anatomy. In doing so, it is meeting genuine needs. Yet many of the images used to market these products seem to rely on familiar, stale clichés that reaffirm patronizing attitudes toward women in sport.

polo, swimming, figure skating, and sailing. Sears also walked a time trial from Boston to Providence in nine hours and fifty-three minutes. By the 1920s, Americans called tennis champion Helen Wills the "New Woman"—and they knew her as well as they knew Babe Ruth.

In the market for some personal renewal themselves, political leaders like Teddy Roosevelt promoted organized sport for the specific purpose of societal regeneration, associating sport with nationalism, character building, and disciplinary and moral value. Men have used sport traditionally as an implement of social design, a way to preserve traditional values against the challenge of change. At the century's turn, male leaders pointed to sport as a way to renew both individual physicality and a nation's energy, thereby securing their hold on the reins of a society on the run. They could justify such claims for sport, ironically enough, partly because casual sport seemed to make women so suddenly healthy. Back in the 1830s, female physical educators, most notably Mary Lyons and Catherine Beecher, surveyed women's health around the country and were shocked to discover how sickly so many women were. Lyons founded Mount Holyoke College, where she instituted mandatory exercise programs, and Beecher wrote a calisthenics book that was implemented for girls throughout the United States. By 1890, their work had paid off: eighty-five thousand women were attending college by then, compared to eleven thousand in 1870, and daily exercise was part of their education.

But later, once sport became culturally entrenched, and after it was assimilated into military training and the business and entertainment industries, women were denied full participation. The emphasis on sport as exclusively a masculinity-defining ritual—as a way to renew male physicality and regenerate manhood—occurred after women demonstrated genuine athletic prowess. As women started to run fast and compete well during the twenties, the first golden age of women's sports, they were summarily shunted to the sidelines. By the thirties, they were no longer welcome. Inter-scholastic and intercollegiate competition for women was cut short after female basketball games started outdrawing boy's and men's games in some high schools and colleges. Females were directed out of baseball and into softball beginning in 1933, after demonstrating their skills in hardball—a seventeen-year-old female pitcher, Jackie Mitchell, struck out Babe Ruth in a promotional event in 1927, for example. And women's opportunities to earn a living at sport were severely limited as men's professional leagues gained and grew. Sport had inclusive, participatory beginnings, but when it became valuable to society, it became a male preserve.

For men, sport carries traditional associations with social and cultural power; for women, it has meant personal liberation and freedom—though on an individual rather than societal level. With this gender definition intact, sport developed throughout the twentieth century as a cultural institution, maintaining its own status quo while seeming to shift to accommodate change. Sport is famous for providing a way for members of the "underclass" to pull themselves up by their bootstraps, and the social structures of sports have opened doors for lower economic classes and ethnic minorities. The last to go is the gender barrier. When Title IX was signed into Federal law in 1972, it was legislation designed in part to ensure that female athletic programs in schools provide the same opportunities as those for males. But even today, some twenty-five years later, examples of discrimination toward female athletes at every level abound. The playing field has not leveled. And despite the athletic freedom women are enjoying today, this personal, physical empowerment has not yet translated into political power.

The path of the American woman is cluttered today by conflicting road signs, her movements guided and monitored by advertisers, sponsors, and a media largely oblivious to her history. Today's golden age of women's sports, which began in the early seventies, is not the first, but the second. The contemporary woman athlete can look back a century to her predecessors in the first heyday for sportswomen, which began in the 1890s. She, too, seemed to be a harbinger of female freedom riding on the back of technological progress.

Notes

1. Tegla Loroupe, interviews Diana Nyad, 12 and 13 December 1996, 3 January 1997.

2. J. B. Strasser and Laurie Becklund, *Swoosh: The Unauthorized Story of Nike, and the Men Who Played There* (New York: Harcourt Brace Jovanovich, 1991).

3. "Adult Foot Structure," *Sport Research Review* (internal publication of Nike, Inc., Beaverton, OR), August/November 1990.

4. "Great Gear," *Women's Sports and Fitness Magazine* (Buyer's Guide), March 1997.

5. Amy Buckalter, interview with Diana Nyad, 2 February 1997.

6. Quoted in "Great Gear."

7. Jay T. Kearney, "Training of the Olympic Athlete," *Scientific American*, June 1996.

8. Linda Lindquist, interview with Diana Nyad. Lindquist was a member of the America3 team.

9. Sara J. Crawley, "Gender and the Perception of Masculinity in Professional Sailing: The Case of the America3 Women's Team" (Ph.D. diss., Florida Atlantic University, 1996).

10. Ibid.

11. "Study on Recent Sports Participation by Women," Sporting Goods Manufacturers Association (SGMA), North Palm Beach, FL, 25 June 1996.

12. John Hoberman, *Mortal Engines: The Science of Performance and the Dehumanization of Sport* (New York: The Free Press, 1992).

13. Ibid.

14. Ibid.

15. Gai Ingham Berlage, *Women in Baseball: The Forgotten History* (Westport, CT: Praeger, 1994).

16. Michael Messner, interview with Diana Nyad, 22 January 1997. Messner is Professor of Sociology and Sport at the University of Southern California.

The Athlete Relocated

AKIKO BUSCH

THE MUSIC ON THE SOUND SYSTEM begins with tranquil new age mood music. The lights are down, and some forty participants are warming up on stationary bikes. The instructor speaks in soothing tones, encouraging them to begin slowly. Within minutes, the tempo will pick up, and the team of indoor cyclists will be pedaling more energetically, the room vibrating with their collective rhythm. The location is the indoor stationary cycling class, one of the most popular offered at New York City's Reebok Club, a high-end fitness training center. The ingredients of this indoor cycling program are stationary bikes, pop music, an instructor who seems equal parts fitness trainer, dj, and drill sergeant. Music ranges from atonal synthetic music to rock with a pounding beat. The imagined landscape is also diverse; as an assortment of hills and flats are called out by the instructor, participants are required to adjust the degrees of resistance on their bikes.

Though stationary cycling has existed for many years, specific fitness programs designed for stationary bikes were not established until 1994, when Mad Dogg athletics introduced it's trademarked Spinning program. Indoor stationary cycling is, of course, based on conventional outdoor bicycling. Traditional stationary exercise bikes, however, are only distant cousins to standard outdoor road bikes; the most obvious difference is that the former don't generally have wheels; resistance is built into the pedal mechanism. But the stationary bikes used for indoor cycling fitness classes have been modified to simulate more closely outdoor racing bikes.

Spinning® exercise program, Culver City, CA (1995). This Spinning class, taught by program inventor Johnny G, is thought by some to be "an indoor Tour de France." Courtesy Mad Dogg Athletics, Inc.

A heavy front or fly wheel is weighted to create momentum that keeps the pedals—directly attached to the wheel—rotating, and the pedals themselves are designed to allow cyclists to extend their legs fully. Multiposition handlebars can accommodate riding in or out of the saddle. And both the form of the saddle and the toe clips provided to help maintain stability were adapted from racing bikes. Finally, the varied ride called out by the instructor—"Okay, slower now, were going up a hill"—also makes for a

Johnny G Spinner® Pro exercise bicycle (1994).
This Schwinn fitness bike takes its cues from a road bike and includes a road-racing bicycle chain, 38-pound cast flywheel, and multiposition handlebars. Courtesy Schwinn and Mad Dogg Athletics, Inc.

workout that is less predictable than that offered by a preprogrammed stationary bike. All of which prompts one advocate to call the class "an indoor Tour de France."

The resemblance to real biking ends there. In an effort to increase the cardiovascular workout, the instructor frequently calls out upper-body exercises, and participants stretch, reach, and otherwise exercise their arms in a manner that would be perilous in traditional outdoor biking, where holding onto the handlebars remains generally advisable. The indoor cyclists also frequently close their eyes. The course doesn't include curved roads, potholes, traffic lights, or buses. Instead, the combination of music, low lighting, and mirrored walls create an atmosphere of unreality that seems somehow appropriate to the activity. Indoor cycling programs occupy some nether realm of exercise—somewhere between a bike ride imagined by Stanley Kubrick and the real thing.

Indeed, the term coined by Mad Dogg for its program says it all. Spinning. For what participants are turning, just as surely as the wheels of their stationary bikes, are notions of indoor and out, nature and artificiality, real and unreal. Indoor stationary cycling may well represent the way we approach sports in the 1990s, and The Johnny G Spinner Pro, the Schwinn stationary bicycle used for the workout and named for its trainer/designer, is a piece of equipment that clearly reflects these ambiguities. The slick geometry of its racing design and its various cycling components reflect a recognition of how sports have been traditionally practiced outdoors—and how those traditions are evolving. Indeed, the variety of sports equipment available today suggests that skills in negotiating the natural world are essential to the overall fitness of the contemporary athlete.

Historically, sports have been practiced outdoors. Today, however, exercise machines, synthetic climbing walls, and a host of other virtual sports equipment all relocate, and at times dislocate, the athlete; they are pieces of equipment that often function as instruments we use to negotiate and revise our relationship to nature. Indeed, for all their precisely calibrated parts, their balance, resilience, and strength, what this equipment may enable us to do most skillfully is balance a profoundly ambiguous—and at times confusing—view of the natural world.

This ambiguity may have its roots in televised sporting events. Televised images give fans an unprecedented proximity to sporting events, allowing viewers to witness more precisely the swing of a tennis racket, the tackle of a quarterback, the split-second slide into second base. In golf, the TV camera delivers viewers right onto the putting green. In baseball, the camera can do even more: it can zoom in on the pitcher on the mound, focus on his grip of the baseball—obscured from the batter by the pitcher's glove—and predict whether he'll throw a fastball or a curve, allowing viewers to know seconds before the batter what the pitch will be, thus transforming entirely the narrative suspense of the game. Such proximity only enhances the viewer's experience of the game.

But aside from proximity, instant replays, the expressions and gestures of professional athletes when they succeed—or fail—to make an important play, the halftime interviews with players, interpretations of controversial referees' calls, and the announcers' commentaries have all become part of the game. Today some fans go to the stadium with portable television sets to watch the game on the screen and on the field simultaneously. And we have come to accept the fact that, while a twelve-inch, two-dimensional TV screen in some way distances us from the three-dimensional reality of the game, the electronic translation of the game also confers its own intimacy. Or, to put it another way, the camera makes it more real. Televised sporting events introduced us to the idea that the mediated event brings us closer to the truth; proximity is both enhanced and diminished, thereby suggesting that ambiguity may be a condition for the spectator's enjoyment of sports.

But our contemporary paradoxical view of nature and sport has precedence on the actual playing fields as well. Traditional upper-class sports such as skiing and golf have both cultivated their own illusionary relationships with the natural world. Golfers often speak of the pleasures of practicing their sport outdoors, extolling the fresh air and stroll across the grassy eighteen-hole course as though it were an excursion through the realm of nature. But the landscape on which they practice their sport has, of course, been precisely engineered, and the elitism and luxury that have been traditionally associated with golf are in part derived from the great cost required to construct and maintain such highly artificial and vast terrain.

Sculpted by bulldozers and earth moving equipment and maintained by elaborate irrigation networks, golf courses rely upon the lavish exploitation of natural resources and extensive use of pesticides, all of which can have significant impact on neighboring environments. Whether it is because golf course designers intend to manufacture a challenging course or to entertain the imagination of players, an afternoon on the links may frequently be an excursion to a fantasy landscape. Among the design features offered by legendary golf course designer Desmond Muirhead at the Aberdeen course in Boynton Beach, Florida, is the Marilyn Monroe

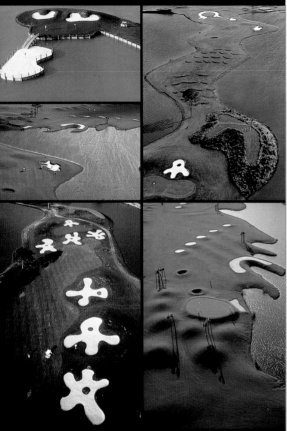

**Aberdeen Golf Course, Boynton Beach, FL
(1986).** While golfers may be accustomed to thinking
of their sport as a sojourn in nature, such precisely
sculpted landscapes as Desmond Muirhead's Aberdeen
Golf Course illustrate the exotic artificiality of the terrain. Courtesy Transeastern properties of Southern
Florida, Inc.

hole, composed of two immense breastlike mounds.
Another hole, when viewed from the air, resembles a
mermaid, a forked tee forming her tail and a pot
bunker positioned at her presumed navel.[1]

Though picturesque in a different way, the
synthetic ski slope demands even greater industrial
intervention, and in recent decades has anticipated
further the revised relationship with nature we
are engaged in today. In his essay "The Nature of
Reality and the Reality of Nature," Albert Borgmann
catalogs the industry of the ski slope:

> A high-speed chairlift scooped you up, rushed
> you along, and deposited you gently. Now you
> are flying down a run that has been cleared of
> trees and rocks, reshaped by bulldozers, and
> planted in grass. Underground there are miles of
> lines for water and compressed air, connected to
> snowguns that line the side of the run. At the
> bottom of the hill, a pumphouse and a compres-
> sor building supply water and air that, guided
> and monitored by computers, are mixed by the
> guns into the quality and quantity of snow
> needed at the time. It has taken a $20 million
> system with a thousand snow guns to produce
> the snow at a cost of $2,700 per acre-foot. But
> this is not all. An army of snow cats, $150,000
> apiece, has worked all night to groom the slope
> to the shape of an undulating corduroy-surfaced
> ballroom floor.[2]

So advanced has the ski industry become,
Borgmann notes, that genuine snow can even
be the object of disdain, thwarting drivers from
faraway urban areas and otherwise simply being
too messy.[3]

Nevertheless, for all the industrial interven-
tions that have gone into the construction of these

artificial landscapes, generations of skiers have maintained the illusion that these mountains are part of the natural environment and that skiing down them provides a sojourn to the extremes of nature in climate and height alike. Today, however, such illusions are no longer necessary. We embrace artificiality more wholeheartedly and more directly.

From the beginning, artificiality was an essential component to the cultural, social, and artistic revolutions of the early twentieth century that became known as the modern movement. The mass production espoused by modernists was fueled by a humanitarian ethos—the belief that new, "artificial" materials and technology could make available more goods for more people at lower cost. But if some modern architects and designers were driven by the vision of a new social order, the fervor of their beliefs was matched by new energy in the corporate laboratories that produced a catalog of new materials during the twenties, thirties, and forties. By the late forties, plastics in the form of cellulose acetate, Plexiglas, vinyl compounds, polystyrene, and polyethylene were reshaping our tableware, appliances, and furnishings. Our homes and offices were sheathed in vinyl, our clothes woven from synthetic threads of nylon, rayon, viscose.

Yet human tastes being what they are, the very nature of the synthetic material—its relative indestructibility, its permanence, its availability—have all been cause for its diminishing appeal. As its material cost decreased, so too did appreciation of the material, until the term "plastic" came to mean commonplace, contrived, insubstantial. The disposability of plastic objects, once meant to be liberating, was interpreted as insufficient, superficial. The countercultural ethos—as opposed to the mainstream perspective—of the sixties and seventies was the

abhorrence of inorganic materials. All manner of synthetic materials were interpreted as counterfeit goods, the dubious rewards of scientific sorcery and metaphors for cultural fraudulence at large.

Today, however, the effort to get back to nature has itself become suspect, simply because there is less of nature to get back to. We have recognized the frailties of our ecology and accepted that our environment is increasingly endangered, its organic materials precious and to be used sparingly; if we are to demonstrate our respect for the natural world, it is by ceasing our reckless exploitation of its materials. Our rampant consumerism has produced mountains of synthetic refuse to which a burgeoning recycling industry must now address itself. Not surprisingly, then, we find ourselves reconsidering the moral value of plastics, and the very qualities of plastics we once despised—endurance, disposability, inorganic sources—all give us cause to accept them. A sweater made from recycled soda bottles is worn as an emblem of social conscience, and a moral value has attached itself to wearing such synthetic apparel; microfiber has a political and cultural cache that polyester did not. We have become open to the possibilities today of recognizing in plastics the integrity we once valued in organic materials; and we have come to accept artificiality as a way of expressing our commitment to the conservation movement.

But it is on the landscape of contemporary sports equipment that the rewards of the artificial realm proliferate most obviously. Machines that enable us to row boats, ski across fields, and ride bicycles in our living rooms all attest to a radically reconstructed relationship with the natural world. More to the point, as the manufacturers of this equipment are fond of pointing out, practicing these sports indoors is often an improvement on

the original activity. In 1911 Edward Chauncey Worden, preeminent historian of the celluloid age, remarked that "the manufacture of cellulose nitreate-camphor containing plastics is essentially an imitative industry and a forgery of many of the necessities and luxuries of civilized life. But unlike many forgeries, these plastics possess properties superior to those of the originals which they are intended to simulate."[4] Similarly, many of the imitations of outdoor exercise that we participate in today are perceived to enhance the original.

Certainly we accept the fact that the simulation of fitness machines often provides a better workout because it can be more effectively regulated. Cross-country skiing, for example, frequently offers a more strenuous workout indoors than out. By regulating the rhythmic patterns of cross-country skiing, indoor fitness equipment not only simulates the sport, but upgrades the workout it offers. Outdoors, the movements are regular and fluid, but only to a point; the skier might pause or swerve to avoid a rock, slow to take in a glimpse of deer in the woods, speed up, and cease the workout altogether when going downhill. While the skier's movements are rhythmic, they are not precisely regulated. Indoors, however, the skier's movements become more mechanical and repetitive. The equipment can be adjusted to various degrees of resistance, and the upper-body workout is improved as well by a mechanism that also offers various degrees of resistance. The smooth motions and domestic landscape of the workout, while not eliminating the threat of injury altogether, surely limit it.

Just as NordicTrack—a leading manufacturer of indoor exercise equipment—has translated cross-country skiing to the indoors, it has looked to other forms of outdoor exercise as well: its WaterRower

TOP: **WaterRower (1987).** With a flywheel that has been built into a water tank, the WaterRower duplicates both the physical exercise of rowing and its attendant sounds of rippling water. Courtesy WaterRower Inc., Warren, RI

ABOVE: **NordicTrack WalkFit 5000.** Indoor power walking is the objective of NordicTrack's Walkfit 5000. Used by permission of NordicTrack, Inc., Chaska, Minnesota, U.S.A.

exerciser has been outfitted with a flywheel built into a tank of water on the theory that both real water resistance and the audio feedback of the sounds of water give the workout greater authenticity. The company's Walkfit exerciser is a fitness machine for simple walking, but because it regulates the movements, it burns more calories, thereby providing a more effective workout than, say, walking around the block. Ergonomic armpoles also ensure a complete upper-body workout.

Similarly, Reebok's Sky Walker not only eliminates the need of going outdoors, it also eliminates the need to ever hit the ground: the exerciser stabilizes the body and allows arms and legs to swing in natural curves without ever making impact. The exercise has been called "vertical swimming," though contact with water is, of course, precluded. The appeal of these walking machines isn't due solely to the regulated workout they offer. The cache of a costly machine to assist us in an exercise for which the mechanics of the human body have traditionally been sufficient may lie in the fact that its indoor workout acknowledges feelings of insecurity and vulnerability. For a population that feels threatened by the increasingly chaotic and violent world outdoors, exercising indoors is simply safer.

The simulated realm offered by fitness equipment has reached a new dimension with advances of interactive software. And if increased safety and more strenuous exercise are two reasons we are inclined to accept these simulations of rowing, skiing, and cycling, entertainment is another. Consider Computrainer, a computer bicycle training system with an interactive video display on which the cyclist can keep his eyes on the road. The stationary bike unit is hooked up to a computer monitor and

CompuTrainer (1986). This computer controlled, electro-mechanical bicycle can be combined with software for video racing. Courtesy Racermate

The cache of a costly machine to assist us in an exercise for which the mechanics of the human body have traditionally been sufficient may lie in the fact that its indoor workout acknowledges feelings of insecurity and vulnerability. For a population that feels threatened by the increasingly chaotic and violent world outdoors, exercising indoors is simply safer.

Life Fitness (1995). The exertainment system by Life Fitness offers users the options of watching TV, the Lifecycle program screen, or a video game, all while working out on a fitness bike. Courtesy Life Fitness

Cardio Theater (1989).
Cardio Theatre brings entertainment to the fitness club. Offering sixteen channels, Australian Body Works of Stone Mountain, Georgia epitomizes the notion of "exertainment." Courtesy Cardio Theater

Life Fitness Rower (1996). Rowers using the Life Fitness Rower and Total Body Conditioner can watch a video with a pace boat, competing rowers, helicopters, and, finally, a threatening shark. Courtesy Life Fitness

allows users to design their own courses with specific grades and road conditions—an advantage to professional cyclists who want to train for specific tours and races that may be many months and thousands of miles away. Cyclists can program in their own weight and the weight of their equipment. Desirable outdoor conditions such as head winds, tail winds, road grade, hills, and flats can be programmed into the course as well. Undesirable conditions, such as wet roads or traffic, are not, again underscoring the intrinsic safety of indoor exercise. The electronic bike trainer offers the realism of the open road without its more distracting components.

The program comes supplied with a "pacer" as well, an electronic biking companion that can interject the competitive element into the workout. With the pacer called up on the screen, the user is challenged further as his electronic opponent makes moves to overtake him. While logistics have heretofore prevented competitive bike racing from moving indoors, with the advent of the modem this is no longer the case.

The computer monitor offers a constant stream of information, cataloging such facts as calories burned, power exerted, target heart rate, speed maintained, and distance covered. Along with the constantly changing degrees of resistance, such information keeps the cyclists from getting bored; some users go so far as to say the ride offered by Computrainer is more interesting and varied than a ride on the open road, simply because so much more information is offered.

The intersection of sports and entertainment is, of course, nothing new. While the Victorians first advocated physical activity as a moral exercise, discipline and health soon became secondary to the sheer pleasures of bicycle riding, swimming, and mountain climbing. Sports became less about pursuing adventure and more about enjoying the pleasures of recreation. Today, we find that recreation evolving increasingly into entertainment; and that entertainment value is often in direct proportion to detachment from the natural world. Increasingly, sports technology and entertainment technology appear to merge gracefully and effortlessly. The constant influx of information on a monitor such as Computrainer keeps serious athletes in training from getting bored while going through the routine motions of a workout. But the boredom of repetitive actions discourage recreational athletes as well; and fitness machine manufacturers point out the advantages of timing your workout with your favorite TV show, suggesting that television may be a motivating factor in exercise routines. This coincidence of voyeuristic entertainment and strenuous physical activity, of course, precludes any interaction with nature although the exercise itself may be based on sports conceived to be practiced in the outdoors.

As interactive equipment becomes more sophisticated, the entertainment options multiply. Recognizing that health and fitness centers may be competing with restaurants and movie theaters for consumer dollars, the fitness industry has, in fact, coined the term "Exertainment" to describe customized interactive equipment that has entertainment value. Cardio Theatre, for example, offers a host of television and audio programs through fitness equipment mounted with selectors. With headphones, users can customize their programming during their cardiovascular workout. And Life Fitness offers a system that combines stationary cycling equipment with a program screen; video games, training feedback, or a combination of TV shows (one viewed on a large screen, while a second can be seen on a smaller window) can all be called up on the screen. "Up close and personal" is how the company defines its product.

For all the entertainment offered by interactive fitness equipment, virtual sports equipment removes the user even further from the natural landscape. Sports museums and halls of fame today invariably provide some kind of virtual sport demonstration that enables viewers to share the experience of champion athletes. Such virtual demonstrations were often originally designed to serve as training tools for athletes, but their entertainment value has since superseded their value as training equipment. Consider the MIR Corporation's Power Alley, a video batting system that is used by such Major League teams as the Texas Rangers, Minnesota Twins, and St. Louis Cardinals—along with the Louisville Slugger Museum in Louisville, Kentucky—to entertain fans.

Power Alley is designed to give museum viewers an experience similar to what the batter experiences at the plate. Viewers stand behind a Plexiglas screen approximately 12 feet in front of a video monitor with the image of a pitcher who then throws a 90-mile-per-hour fastball to a model of a catcher positioned directly in front of the viewer and screen. Balls can be thrown by a generic pitcher or from pros like Roger Clemens, Hideo Nomo, and Mike Mussina. (The MIR camera team has filmed over 200 professional pitchers during regular season games and is in the process of editing their pitches and transferring them to laser disc to be included in the system.) Also programmed into the system is the time taken between pitches. Announcements are displayed on a computer clipboard and a sound system reproduces the roar of the crowd.

Similarly, at the Basketball Hall of Fame in Springfield, Massachusetts, one of the most popular displays is a virtual reality fantasy basketball

demonstration that offers viewers the chance to shoot hoops with Bill Walton. Participants stand in front of a blue screen upon which their image is superimposed and mixed with digitally stored footage of Walton. Viewers devise their own plays using a small monitor placed in front of them that displays images of the ball and Walton. The computer registers the height and hand position of the viewer, returning the ball to the correct place on the screen after each scrimmage. A large overhead screen allows other museum viewers to watch the simulated game.

The irony, of course, is that such virtual experiences can, in fact, make the traditionally distanced spectator more physically and spatially aware of what the professional athlete experiences. In much the same way that television footage brings the viewer into closer proximity to sporting events, virtual demonstrations such as these confer their own peculiar brand of intimacy.

Power Alley carries a price tag close to $90,000, but video games available at a substantially lower cost enable one to play virtual sports at home. Consider Batter Up, a video batting game designed for home use. Here, a 24-inch foam-covered electronic bat is equipped with transmitters that are compatible with Sega Genesis or Super Nintendo games. A pitcher on a TV screen pitches the ball, and the batter's swing is recorded, with the final speed, distance, and position of the ball appearing on the screen.

Similarly, the ProSwing system is a training tool that allows home golfers to tee off in their living rooms. Its components include a 26-inch club—that has been engineered to replicate the feel of a conventional club—and a base unit containing electronic circuits and sensors. A light in the shape of a specified club head is emitted from the bottom of

CLOCKWISE FROM TOP LEFT:

Batter Up (1993). Batter Up is a 24-inch electronic bat compatible with video game systems. After plugging the unit in, players can face down pitches from the TV set. Courtesy Sports Sciences Inc.

Virtual Basketball (1992). Visitors to the Basketball Hall of Fame in Springfield, Massachusetts are invited to play one-on-one Virtual Basketball with legend Bill Walton. Courtesy Basketball Hall of Fame

Power Alley (1991). The Power Alley Video Batting System gives players the experience of facing down a 90-mile-per-hour fastball. Courtesy the MIR Corporation, Lilburn, Georgia

the club; it can be changed by a dial on the club from a driver head to a long iron to a short iron to a putter. When the golfer swings, the base unit then records the light from the club and analyzes such information as the position of the club face at impact; the distance the ball has traveled in yards or meters; the club speed in miles or kilometers per hour; and the flight path of the ball, from severe slice to severe hook. A built-in sound system also replicates the various sounds of the driver, iron, and putter hitting the ball. While the system can be used as a stand-alone training device, it can also be hooked up to a PC, with software that allows users to play a full eighteen-hole course with a driving range, chipping green, and putting green. Additional software for specific championship courses from Florida to Hawaii is also available with full graphics representing their verdant landscapes.

If ProSwing was designed as a training tool, PC Golf puts a higher value on the entertainment factor. Rather than analyzing the swing, PC Golf is a system that provides an electronic 26-inch club and a sensor pad with microprocessors and golf ball graphics. When connected to computer software, it enables home golfers to view the speed, angle, and distance of the electronic golf ball on a television monitor. Whether such drives, chips, and putts qualify as training or entertainment depends largely on the perception of the user.

The Chelsea Piers Sports and Entertainment Complex, a veritable sports mall in New York City, offers yet another golfing environment—a year-round, multilevel driving range on a pier that stretches into the Hudson river. Fifty-two heated and weather-protected hitting stalls have been stacked in four tiers. Computerized automatic ball transport systems deliver balls from ground level to these tee stations, where automatic teeing allows

PC Golf (1990). PC Golf offers interactive golf for home or office; the flight path of the ball "hit" with a 26-inch club is recorded on a computer monitor. Courtesy Sports Sciences Inc.

Driving range at Chelsea Piers, New York (1997). The golf club at Chelsea Piers, a 30-acre "sports village" in New York City, offers fifty-two individual stalls stacked alongside a heated driving range and mechanical tees. Courtesy Fred George

golfers to program individual tee heights before driving balls across the 200-yard range surfaced with artificial turf. Periodically throughout the day, a small cart roams the turf, vacuuming up balls to be delivered back to the tunnels and chutes of the transport system. At the Chelsea Piers range, golfers not only needn't walk; they don't even have to bend over to position balls on the tee: the mechanized tee manages that task for them. Polyethylene netting to prevent balls from straying into river traffic hangs from a series of twelve 160-foot-tall black steel towers that sit on pilings some of which descend 280 feet into the river's bedrock. (For all the technological innovation of the driving range, however, it's interesting to note that the design of the white clapboard golf house maintains a tenacious hold on the culture of golf, conveying a more anachronistic identity: its shingles, portico, white interior wainscoting, and low ceilings all suggest the cozy and genteel elitism of the traditionally exclusive New England country club.)

Whether it is the spectacular driving range of Chelsea Piers or computerized golfing, what these options offer golfers, of course, is not limited to the opportunity to drive balls year round; they also suggest that the sport can be socially repositioned. Eliminated are the traditional camaraderie and exercise golfers associate with their sport. But by also eliminating the need for vast amounts of outdoor space that require constant and meticulous grooming, they reduce the traditional elitism of the sport. Golfers no longer need necessarily to travel to the suburbs or apply to exclusive clubs to lower their handicaps. So in the process of relocation from its traditional acreage of well tended and artificially constructed and maintained courses to an even more artificial realm, the sport becomes more egalitarian, accessible to a wider population.

While fitness equipment, interactive virtual sports demonstrations, and synthetic driving ranges surely manage to reconfigure every manner of outdoor exercise, some also go so far as to simulate the atmosphere as well. Consider indoor skydiving—even its name is a mind-boggling contradiction of terms. Such an assault on logic nevertheless occurs regularly in Las Vegas at Flyaway, a 22-foot vertical wind tunnel; its airspeed of 110 miler per hour eliminates the need for both airplane and sky, components that have traditionally been necessary to the practice of skydiving. Indoor parachutists are encouraged to "achieve the dream" of human flight; wearing flight suits and helmets they can rent the room for hour-long "flights" during which they can simply practice maneuvers or film their "flights" on video for later analysis. Team building exercises are offered, as are flight parties. There are no bad weather days in tunnel flying, no cumbersome parachute rigs to pack, and, clearly, no danger of falling thousands of feet to one's death: there is simply the experience of being afloat.

The fitness club Crunch in New York City tours a different high atmosphere, offering an oxygen-depleted environment for athletes in training for events in high altitude regions. "Crunch brings the mountain to the gym," says the promotional material for the Hypoxic Room System, an 8 x 8 foot vinyl chamber that simulates the oxygen level of a 9,000 foot-high mountain such as one might find in the Rockies or Sierras. Unhealthy air components—ozone, for example—are not replicated.

FACING PAGE: **Flyaway (1980–81).** Indoor skydiving at Flyaway in Las Vegas efficiently reduces the risk of the sport by eliminating the need for the plane, the parachute, and even the sky. Courtesy Flyaway

Hypoxic Room System (1995). The Hypoxic Room System offers an oxygen depleted environment more traditionally found at a 9,000 foot elevation. Courtesy Hypoxico, Inc.

the body to function well on the low-oxygen content of mountain air, physical performance in a more regular environment will also be improved.

It's one thing to bring mountain air into the gym at sea level; it's quite another to bring the mountain itself, but that's the objective in the relatively recent industry of synthetic wall climbing. Artificial surfaces have extended the possibilities of sports since the Houston Astrodome was constructed in 1965. Its nine acres of playing field in an air-conditioned interior were spanned by a clear, louvered Lucite roof. A team of botanists from Texas A&M specified a strain of grass for the outfield that could grow with 20 percent reduced light. But for the more heavily trafficked infield, stadium developers looked not to botanists but to the Chemstrand Corporation for a nylon monofilament woven into a polyester backing with a second backing of vinyl chloride for additional cushioning.[5] The AstroTurf, as this new surfacing material was known, was so green that the sod outfield was painted to match before the first game. Almost since its first appearance, however, artificial turf has raised complaints from athletes about sports injuries caused by its relatively unresistant surface—research suggests that foot and knee injuries may occur as much as 50 percent more often on artificial turf than on grass. All the same, its low maintenance costs continue to ensure its appeal, and all types of artificial turf have been laid down since the mid-sixties in stadiums and arenas around the country.

As a surface that mediates our contact with the natural world, however, artificial turf was just the beginning. The art and industry of artificial surfaces reached a new dimension with the development of synthetic climbing walls in the mid-seventies. First designed in Europe as an adjunct training device for

Athletes acclimate to the room by exercising in it for five minutes, followed by five minutes of rest outside the room in five or six cycles per workout session. While the original purpose of the Hypoxic Room was to train athletes—skiers, boxers, swimmers, cyclers, runners, tennis players—to compete in high altitude regions, it is now being used as a more general fitness conditioning tool. High-altitude exercise lowers the heart rate and breathing frequency, and athletes accustomed to performing in high altitudes generally have better endurance than athletes from lower altitudes. By conditioning

outdoor climbers, synthetic climbing soon helped to change the very nature of the sport, affecting both the skill and ethos associated with traditional alpine and rock climbing.

Interior climbing has helped to popularize climbing, and in the process has significantly changed the way the sport is practiced. The concrete polymer used to fabricate most of these walls can be made in panels or to conform to larger, more idiosyncratic shapes. Either way, the material can be easily altered to form any angle of slope, ledge, or overhang, providing climbing routes that require varying degrees of technical skill. Likewise, polyester resin holds can be easily adjusted and moved to mark routes of varying difficulty. Because specific routes can be so easily designed and constructed, indoor climbing lends itself to competitions more so than outdoor climbing; and competitions help to popularize any sport. Add to that the fact that outdoor climbing necessitates a degree of trail erosion and wildlife disturbance, and indoor climbing holds out a moral value as well.

The popularization of the sport has changed it in numerous ways. For safety, indoor routes are usually top-roped from a metal bar overhead, and today top-roping is generally more acceptable outdoors as well. Because it is difficult to reproduce the cracks one finds on rock in synthetic walls, techniques developed to deal with these cracks are not easily learned indoors. Climbing professionals also often refer to a diminished recognition of risk on the part of indoor climbers. Climbers who learn their skills indoors without confronting extreme heights or inclement weather may have an inflated sense of their abilities and fail to recognize the very different risks posed by outdoor climbing. At the same time, indoor climbing has proved a benefit to the sport: the availability of synthetic walls that can be used all year

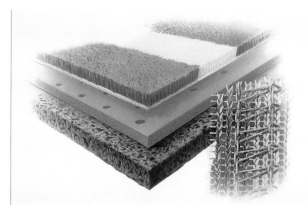

AstroTurf 2000 (1996). The most recent and advanced generation of AstroTurf is the multilayered AstroTurf 2000, constructed of (from the bottom up): a rubber or rubber and stone sub-base; a layer of closed cell foam; and texturized fibers for uniform traction and correct ball roll properties. Courtesy Summit Communications, Arlington Heights, IL

has allowed many rock climbers to train more intensely. And overhangs, unusual in outdoor rock formations, can be easily constructed indoors, allowing climbers to practice and master such gravitational challenges, thereby raising considerably standards of both technical skill and climber physical fitness.

But synthetic climbing walls have not simply changed the sport of climbing. They have created their own new, independent sport that dovetails neatly with the fitness industry. Climbing offers a total body workout that includes endurance, flexibility, and aerobics. Consider Treadwall, a combination fitness machine and climbing wall that represents this intersection of activities. Called "a precision rock climbing simulator," Treadwall is constructed of panels of textured fiberboard that are made to rotate, like a conventional treadmill, by body weight. The angle or slope of the unit can be easily adjusted, while color-coded holds indicate a variety of routes.

Treadwall (1989). Both the angle and climbing route—marked by forty-two modular climbing holds—of Treadwall can be easily adjusted to offer a nearly limitless variety of indoor climbs. An automatic counter affixed to the unit measures time, feet climbed, and calories burned. Courtesy Brewer's Ledge Inc.

As its promotional literature attests, users "get all the benefits of mountain climbing without the risk."[6]

While the cost of Treadwall may limit its use to fitness clubs, some inventive climbers have found a different way to hone their skills twenty-four hours a day. By installing polymer climbing holds on load-bearing walls throughout the home, they establish a variety of climbing routes through kitchen, den, and living room. With their range of plastic colors and shapes, these edges, pinches, pockets, and slopers—as the various holds are called—invariably provide an innovative home design motif, not to mention the literal proof that home is a place that can make you climb the walls.

Aside from being suited to competition and aside from addressing the needs of the fitness industry, indoor climbing also values different skills and attributes than traditional climbing. In the words of one climbing aficionado, "Outdoor climbing is about exposure. It's about the human response of not wanting to die. Indoor climbing is essentially safer."[7] With climbing ropes usually top-roped from above, the landing surface is soft and resilient, the heights less daunting. Not surprisingly, then, indoor climbing places fewer psychological demands on the climber: examining one's inner resources is no small part of the challenge in scaling a 500-foot granite ledge, but those resources are simply less relevant indoors. Instead, indoor climbing is more acrobatic. Because one is in an essentially safer position, one hesitates less to leap or spring for a hold that is beyond immediate grasp. An oversize purple polyester resin hold attached to a polymer concrete wall several feet above the floor conveys greater reliability than a crack in a sheer granite slope. Indoor climbing also puts a high value on physical strength. Because challenging overhangs can be easily constructed, difficult routes can be devised that may place strenuous physical demands on the fitness climber.

So popular has indoor climbing become that synthetic walls are being constructed in a variety of unlikely landscapes. Surely the most unusual is Upper Limits, the self-described world's tallest climbing gym. Outgrowing their small indoor climbing gym in Peru, Illinois, owners Chris and Pam Schmick purchased a series of thirteen abandoned cement soybean silos outside Bloomington, Illinois.

They cleaned out the residual rotten soybeans, blasted the walls clean, and installed a variety of climbing routes ranging from 30 to 145 feet by placing some three thousand climbing holds into the cement walls. To sculpt overhanging routes constructed around roof areas, spray-on concrete was used. Depending on local weather conditions—a nod to the sentimental notion that natural climate can be a player in rock climbing—ice climbing is sometimes offered in winter months.

That alpine climbing can be practiced in the flat prairies and cornfields of the Midwest says something about the way we have developed the ability to disregard the confines of the natural world. And like those other sports disciplines mentioned here—like modem biking, virtual baseball, and high-altitude exercise chambers—silo climbing suggests that the conditions of the natural world are becoming increasingly irrelevant to the practice of sport; and that if the conditions set forth by nature don't satisfy, are impractical, or are otherwise inconvenient, we can simply devise a synthetic alternative. It is an approach to sports that would suggest that nature is replaceable, a view that is very possibly consistent with a larger cultural attitude.

In his elegant treatise on the passing of nature, "The End of Nature," Bill McKibben writes that

> Nature has become a hobby with us. One person enjoys the outdoors, another likes cooking, a third favors breaking into military computers over his phone line. The nature hobby boomed during the 1970s; now it is perhaps in slight decline (the number of people requesting permits to hike and camp in the rugged backcountry of national parks has dropped by half since 1983, even as the number of drive-through visitors has continued to increase.) We have become in rapid

LEFT: **Upper Limits Rock Gym, Bloomington, Illinois.** Five abandoned grain silos have been reinvented as Upper Limits Rock Gym, the world's tallest climbing facility. Courtesy Upper Limits

RIGHT: **Ice Climbing at Upper Limits Rock Gym.** In a quaint nod to the conditions of the natural world, the silos of Upper Limits may be transformed to artificial frozen waterfalls for ice climbing in winter months. Courtesy Upper Limits

> order a people whose conscious need for nature is superficial. The seasons don't matter to most of us anymore except as spectacles. In my county and in many places around this part of the nation, the fair that once marked the harvest now takes place in late August, while tourist dollars are still in heavy circulation. Why celebrate the harvest when you harvest every week with a shopping cart?[8]

Insofar as the artifacts of the physical world are documents of our civilization, the sports equipment we use today reaffirms this view that the natural world is disposable. In the landscape of contemporary sports, nature is, if not superfluous, then negotiable. Nature is no longer an absolute that we must confront, but a single component of modern experience, one of many that can be selected on an as-needed or as-wanted basis. Where sports are concerned, the synthetic realm may offer a more rewarding workout; it may be safer, it may be more entertaining, and it may be more egalitarian. Technology has allowed us to break down the components of different sports. The physical activity, the landscape it takes place in, the condition of the terrain, the climate, the feel of the equipment, the sounds of the sport—all of these have traditionally been the conditions that, when added up, define each particular sport.

Today, they can be experienced separately. And they can be manufactured separately so that we can enjoy some components without others. Golf clubs can be reassembled as shafts of light; towers of ice can be sculpted into vertical speed climbing walls without the extremes of wind and temperature associated with conventional Alpine climbing; we can breathe thin mountain air in urban fitness spas and ride bikes on traffic-free video monitors. All of these increase our options. "And our desires count," writes McKibben. "Nothing is necessarily going to force us to live humbly; we are free to chance the other deviant route and see what happens....there is no certainty we must simultaneously cut back on our material desires—not if we're willing to live in a world ever more estranged from nature."[9]

Part of satisfying out material desires is having an ever-expanding range of options. Tucker Viemeister, a creative director for frogdesign in New York City, suggests that the design and technology of sports equipment has not simply allowed new possibilities for the practice of established sports; he also suggests that these allow contemporary

sports to occupy a far broader realm of activity today than they have before. In 1996, Smart Design (for whom Viemeister was then a principal) designed the Alps Interactive Game Pad, a reconfigured controller for video games. With its streamlined form and rubber grips, the controller was marketed as a piece of sports equipment: "As advanced sports medicine shaves nanoseconds off Olympian performance, the embedded ergonomics amplify microfinger movements to actually improve scoring performance," reads its promotional literature.[10] Viemeister suggests that video games indeed qualify as sport. "You can run around with no equipment at all," he says. "Or, sports can be all about the equipment. In my view, the hand/eye coordination and the game aspect of video games qualifies them as sport. Just because you're not using your legs doesn't mean it's not a sport. Video games are as much about sport as football. There, you just have a lot of robots running around. Both of these are all about equipment."[11] That video games qualify as sport may be an extreme view; certainly it is one that reaffirms the estrangement from nature alluded to by McKibben.

That said, the estrangement is not absolute. While the virtual basketball display is one of the most popular exhibits at the Basketball Hall of Fame, curator Mike Brooslin observes that another exhibit consisting of a conveyer belt that delivers real basketballs to visitors so they can shoot real hoops remains by far the best attended. At Chelsea Piers, an effort was made to focus sports and fitness programs on total body activity; while the center does offer an interior climbing wall, there are no virtual sports demonstrations. And at the Reebok Club, sports simulators have been replaced by conventional fitness machines. When the club opened it had installed a MetroSki simulator that pivoted on seven axes, creating G-forces similar to those that might be felt skiing down a mountain. A video monitor placed in front of the skier re-created the slopes of Vail. For those more inclined to warm weather sports, a virtual windsurfing machine could simulate a variety of wind conditions. Both simulation machines have since been replaced by a host of more conventional exercise machines that were in greater demand by clients.

We are all, to some extent, like those rock climbers at Upper Limits who seem so effortlessly to navigate their routes between the natural and artificial realms. The tableau they create is strictly postmodern—climbers in bright Gore-Tex and fleece outerwear hoisting synthetic gear across immense silos. Integrating the traditional monuments of rural America with the contemporary fitness industry, the imagery concocts its own visual logic; and in doing so, boggles the imagination. Indeed, for all the skilled rappelling and climbing at Upper Limits, one of the most graceful and tenacious maneuvers that occurs there—and elsewhere in the landscape of contemporary sports—may be in how the athletes tread that balance between the natural and synthetic realms. And it is a part of our identity as residents of the late twentieth century not to find this disruptive, but rather to accept it, indeed embrace it, as a condition of modern living.

Alps Interactive Game Pad (1996). With its streamlined form, implicit demand for hand/eye coordination, and recognition of the competitive element, the Alps Inter-active Game Pad designed by Smart Design may epitomize the future of sports equipment. Courtesy Smart Design

Notes

1. John Strawn, "Voluptuous Earth," *Metropolis*, July/August 1989, 49.

2. Albert Borgman, "The Nature of Reality and the Reality of Nature," *Reinventing Nature* (Washington, DC: Island Press, 1995), 37.

3. Ibid.

4. Stephen Fenichell, *Plastic: The Making of a Synthetic Century* (New York: HarperCollins, 1996), 12.

5. Ibid., 298.

6. Treadwall brochure, Brewer's Ledge, Inc., Boston, MA, 1994.

7. Eric Reff, interview with the author, Island Rock climbing facility, Plainview, NY, January 1979.

8. Bill McKibben, *The End of Nature* (New York: Anchor Books, 1990), 69.

9. Ibid., 193.

10. "Announcing the End of Video Game Toys," press release, Smart Design, New York, NY, 1996.

11. Tucker Viemeister, telephone interview with the author, 30 January 1997.

Tradition, Talent, and Technology: The Ambiguous Relationship between Sports and Innovation

J. NADINE GELBERG

WHILE TITANIUM BATS, diamond-coated golf clubs, and assorted other space-age materials may suggest that sports welcome technological innovations, sports organizations, in fact, regularly prohibit creative new designs. Although sports are about earning advantages, the performance of human athletic talent remains the core of sport. Preserving this core is the reason that, despite what may appear to be a *laissez-faire* attitude toward innovations, javelins and baseballs do not endlessly soar beyond stadiums, golf balls do not self-correct in flight, and tennis racket strings fail to turn regular top-spin strokes into Björn Borg-caliber shots.

In most endeavors, any technology that improves the efficiency of production is enthusiastically accepted. Sport, however, is unique in that the process is paramount to the product; while we are interested in who gets to the finish line the fastest, how they get there is of equal, if not greater, importance. Runners cannot run across the middle of the track, but must traverse the distance around the track; rowers don't rely on a motor to get to the finish line, nor do rock climbers take helicopters or elevators to reach summits. Such artificial inefficiencies are what test athletic skill and allow for the display of athletic excellence. To retain the essential human element in sport, sports organizations permit those technologies that enable sport participation while banning those that compromise the challenge or tradition of the activity.

While some technologies compromise sporting tradition or athletic challenge, other innovations provide athletes opportunities to display their talents and encourage the sport to grow. Variety in equipment design allows athletes to select that which best complements their abilities. Tennis players with excellent backcourt skills may select a racket that enhances power groundstrokes. Just as different sizes and cuts of clothing fit different people, different equipment designs complement different mixes of athletic talent. Providing a level playing field requires athletes be allowed to select the equipment that allows them to best display their athletic excellence. A greater variety of designs enables more athletes to participate and encourages growth in sport.

Sport technology policy must not only balance sporting tradition, athletic challenge, and technological innovation; it must also consider how technology affects a sport's safety, cost, and image. Although sports organizations try to minimize the risk in sport, all sport involves some risk, and for many the danger is part of the appeal; sports organizations may mandate or ban certain technologies to ensure safety. And while design innovations may enable athletes to use equipment that complements their particular skills, such equipment may also dramatically increase the cost of the sport. If a sport becomes prohibitively expensive, fewer recreational and youth athletes will participate, and spectator interest will wane. Even at the elite level, some countries may end their participation in costly sports. To protect against skyrocketing expenses, sports organizations may prohibit certain innovations.

Sports survive on funding that increases as spectator interest climbs. In determining technology policy, then, sports organizations must consider what equipment makes the game more appealing to spectators—and what detracts from the public image of the sport. One technology may be banned for the same reason another is accepted. Sport technology policy must balance numerous concerns.

Sports organizations have historically implemented ad hoc technological regulations based on design standards when responding to crises and perceived threats to the integrity of the sports they govern. Such regulation of sports equipment involves a complexity of issues, including the consideration of the interests and needs of various groups of athletes (men and women, recreational and professional) and sporting goods manufacturers, as well as the affect of the new technology on the sport itself. Will the prohibiting of new equipment be a detriment to popular appeal? Once a decision is made, it can be difficult to retract: for example, after an innovation becomes widely accepted in a sporting community, banning it—after athletes, fans, and manufacturers have invested heavily in it—is difficult indeed. Because sports organizations cannot foresee the future and anticipate all possible materials and designs, creating performance standards, as opposed to design standards, may provide a more prudent strategy. This would protect both tradition and the essential test of sporting skills, while permitting flexibility in equipment innovation.

Sporting Tradition and Baseball Bats

Prohibiting innovation to protect tradition preserves sport as a continuously unfolding story. Unlike most forms of entertainment, in sport fan interest extends beyond the end of a particular event: the final out at the World Series, the crossing of the finish line at a world championship, or the final whistle of the Superbowl. Spectators follow who has been traded and drafted, and who has retired. Enthusiasts compare current records to past achievements and postulate how historic heroes would fare against modern champions. While movies and plays all end, sport continues. Protecting the link with the past is one reason sports organizations ban certain equipment designs.

While the "ping" of an aluminum baseball bat hitting the ball may be applauded in Japanese baseball stadia and accepted in colleges, it is banned in Major League baseball parks. There, bats remain wooden clubs despite the transformation from the wagon-tongue shaped bats A. G. Spalding sold in the 1870s to the scientifically designed modern baseball bat.

According to legend, the Louisville Slugger was born in 1884 when the best hitter on the Louisville Eclipses, Pete Browning, broke his bat. John Hillerich went to his father's wood shop and turned the slugger a new bat on his lathe. Browning's success on the diamond in subsequent outings created a demand for the Louisville Slugger, launching the famous Hillerich & Bradsby Company into the history books and a 98 percent market share prior to the mid-1970s. The wagon tongue days were officially over in 1893 when a ruling designed to promote the "manly" sport and slugging, established that bats be cross-sectionally round—though beyond this, there was room for modification.[1]

Attempts to reduce bat weight led to changes in materials and shapes. Major Leaguers no longer swing heavy hickory clubs, preferring the improved strength-to-weight ratio of white ash. Current wooden bats weigh seven to ten ounces less than the clubs Babe Ruth and his contemporaries used to hit homers.[2] In addition to improved maneuverability, these lighter weights allow Major Leaguers to increase their bat speeds, a crucial factor in the ball's rebound velocity, which determines the distance the ball will travel. In addition to the new type of wood used to reduce bat weight, new shapes with smaller handles and large barrels have also become the norm.[3]

While such bats offer minimum weight and maximum bat speed, they also break easily, posing both safety and cost concerns. While players and spectators regularly watch for fly balls, they are less aware of flying bats. Sluggers such as Pete Incaviglia have used forty dozen bats in a season.[4] The increasing demand for high-quality wooden bats, along with the diminishing supply of good wood, creates an economic problem. The wood used for a Major League bat comes from seventy-five-year-old trees. Once the trees are felled and sliced into 40-inch lengths, the highest quality pieces are split into quarters. Out of one hundred splits, only five to ten will be of sufficient quality to produce Major League bats.[5] The expense, time, and materials necessary to keep professional players supplied with an increasing number of bats has left some of the league's elite players waiting months for their orders to be filled.

For reasons of both cost and skill development, college and little league players do not have to await their wooden weapons—they buy aluminum. On average, Major League teams purchase seven dozen bats per player, per season, eighty-four times the number colleges using aluminum bats buy. By using aluminum bats, which rarely break, colleges can save approximately $10,000 per season.[6] In addition to the dramatic difference in cost and ease in filling orders, aluminum bats allow athletes to maximize their athletic talents.

Successful hitting requires optimizing bat speed and mass with control. Both the bat's weight and distribution of mass are factors in determining the distance the ball will travel. Too heavy a bat will reduce bat speed, while too light a bat may yield an insufficient increase in bat speed to compensate for the reduction of mass. Moreover, a heavy bat is more difficult to control than a lighter bat. To determine the ideal bat weight for each player, an engineering professor at the University of Arizona, Terry Bahill, performed some studies with college players for the Arizona Wildcats. Bahill found that bats between 23.3 and 31.8 ounces were ideal. Unfortunately, these low weights were next to impossible to achieve with wood while maintaining structural integrity.[7]

Aluminum bats also benefit youth leagues. With wood strong enough to withstand the impact of a baseball, 32 ounces is virtually the lowest weight bat available. If all athletes were required to use such heavy bats, only the strongest and biggest would be successful players. Athletes whose skills were greater bat control, hand-eye coordination, reaction time, and bat speed would be at a disadvantage. Moreover, wooden bats have a smaller sweet spot and the vibrations caused by less-than-perfect hits tend to "sting" players' hands. Such "stings" are accentuated in colder climates, making batting practice with wooden bats difficult during the collegiate season for northern schools. The reduced cost and design flexibility of aluminum bats, then, have offered nonprofessional athletes

LEFT: **Titanium Bat (1994).** The materials and form of the baseball bat have been under reconsideration for decades. Both stronger and more flexible than aluminum or carbon fiber versions, titanium baseball bats can add ten to fifteen yards to a batter's range. Such bats, however, are about five times the cost of those used in the Major Leagues. Courtesy Easton Sports

RIGHT: **Cryogenic Baseball Bat (1996).** The cryogenic softball bat has been made with aluminum subjected to temperatures well below zero during the manufacturing process. When metals are cooled, molecular movements are slowed, rendering a structure that is more dense and subsequently more resistant to wear. Courtesy Worth Inc.

the opportunity to fully display and develop their baseball talents.

In 1973 the Baseball Rules Committee for the National Collegiate Athletic Association (NCAA) became concerned about both the cost and quality of their wooden bats. College teams complained that the wood specified for collegiate play was of inferior quality, causing bats to break frequently, and that the increasing numbers of broken bats had become prohibitively costly. The Rules Committee then gave the "okay" for aluminum bat use. The concern over competitive balance was not paramount since the aluminum then in use did not offer hitters a significant advantage. The only real advantage to the 1970 aluminum bats was durability.[8]

Ten years later, the durability and strength of aluminum bats also began to provide performance advantages. With stronger alloys, the bat wall could be made thinner to reduce bat weight. Reduced weight allowed the batter to increase his swing velocity and accuracy, yielding a real hitting advantage. The NCAA responded in 1988 by instituting a rule stating that a bat could be no more than 5 ounces lighter than the bat's length in inches. Thus a 34-inch bat must weigh at least 29 ounces. In 1988 all bats were well within that standard. Yet, less than ten years later, bats manufactured with a variety of materials designed for NASA, the space agency, have sent the NCAA searching for new ways to maintain tradition, encourage safety, and preserve the competitive balance in baseball.[9]

In 1997 the NCAA engaged independent research teams and instituted an interim standard for bat performance that focused on the rebound properties of the baseball bat. It established that a ball cannot rebound more than 15 percent faster off a stationary bat than off a solid wall, thereby checking the trampoline effect from thin-walled bats. This interim standard may soon enter the rule books after independent research helps the NCAA analyze other options for bat performance standards.[10]

Manufacturers and innovators regularly stretch their imaginations to design equipment that will improve performance. Jeffrey DiTullio, an aeronautics instructor at the Massachusetts Institute of Technology, has recently designed a dimpled baseball bat. Like the dimples on the golf ball, the dimples on this bat reduce air resistance and allow for a quicker swing. Though such a bat may improve swing velocity, there are limits to how fast a person's muscles can swing an implement. Regardless, it will not be given the chance in college play. The NCAA requires that the entire bat be round with a constant radius from all points and that the finish of the hitting surface be smooth.[11]

Other innovations have included the installation of a moving mass within the bat. Such a design recognizes the advantage of increased mass at the point of contact. While not increasing weight that hampers swing velocity, it provides a low moment of inertia during swing, but a high moment of inertia at collision. Because the rebound velocity of the ball is determined by the swing velocity and the mass of the contact implement, the ideal implement would be light enough to increase swing velocity, but heavy enough to send the ball soaring. Such a bat is hollowed out, then partially filled with water. During the batter's stance the water, or mass, would remain close to the handle or player's wrists, the axis of rotation; during the swing the water moves out to the barrel, providing additional mass at the contact point with the ball. Predictably, the NCAA forbids any bat modification to improve performance.[12]

Major Leaguers do not, however, share the concerns of the youth and collegiate leagues. Professional teams can afford the high cost of

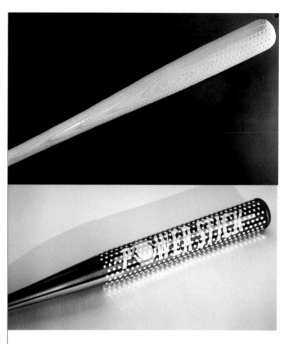

Power Stick Dimpled Bats in Wood and Aluminum (1994). Dimpled bats have been the subject of investigation by Jeffrey DiTullio, an aeronautics instructor at MIT. Because the layer of air next to a moving object moves more slowly than the layer of air immediately above it, an object with an irregular or rough surface—which intermingles these two layers of air—will move through the air more efficiently than a smooth object. Thus, the dimples pressed into the surface of these bats reduce drag. Courtesy Jeffrey DiTullio and MIT

wooden baseball bats. Their players also hit the sweet spot more consistently, not needing a larger ideal hitting space. Finally, they have little need for lighter-weight materials, the ideal weight for a Major League bat being about 30 ounces. For the Major Leagues, wood meets the competitive needs and retains the traditional game of lumber and leather.

The crack of the bat is part of the traditional aura of the game, and remains essential to Major Leaguers and fans of baseball tradition. The literature and history of the sport revolves around the crack of the wooden bat, and the diminished resonance of the aluminum versions would put the game at a further remove from its pastoral origins. Statisticians argue that aluminum bats would dramatically increase batting averages, home run totals, and make existing ballparks obsolete. To preserve the sacred sound, look, and feel of baseball, only solid wood bats have been allowed in the Major Leagues.

Both aluminum and the new realm of composite materials available today are flexible enough to yield radically new bat designs. Indeed, manufacturers can produce a bat that performs and sounds like a wooden bat. Such composites break less often than traditional wood bats yet retain the feel, performance, and sound of the natural club.[13] What will Major League Baseball say to such an innovation—one that retains the traditional sound and look of a wooden bat but with the size, weight, and durability of composites?

> The literature and history of the sport revolves around the crack of the wooden bat, and the diminished resonance of the aluminum versions would put the game at a further remove from its pastoral origins.

Cycling

How tradition has been preserved is altogether different in the sport of cycling. Contemporary bicycles only minimally resemble the Schwinn bikes children raced through the newly built suburbs of the fifties, and even less the wooden and steel "boneshaker" of the 1860s, which men straddled with their feet on the ground and propelled in a walking manner.

Since the invention of the sport, riders have redesigned the bicycle in an effort to increase speed. In 1938 a French rider broke several records racing a recumbent bike. In response, the Union Cycliste Internationale (UCI)—the sport's governing body—banned recumbent bicycles and additions to the bike made solely for the purpose of reducing wind resistance. Although the U.S. Cycling Federation was denied approval by UCI for disk, or "spokeless," wheels in 1982, two years later an Italian set the outdoor record with a radical new vehicle on disk wheels. From noncircular peddling patterns to high angled seats to new materials such as carbon fiber, Kevlar, and titanium, wheelmen have embraced new innovations, though not always with the blessing of the UCI.[14]

The UCI puts a high value on the traditions of cycling. In an October 1996 press release, the UCI defined the bicycle as a "historical phenomenon" and claimed it was "history which underpins the culture behind the technical object."[15] Equally important for the UCI is how the sport tests riders' physical abilities. New designs can transform the sport into tests of engineering rather than sporting talent. In an effort to safeguard the sport, the UCI writes regulations in "keeping with the spirit and principle of cycling" and "asserts the primacy of man over machine."[16]

Not surprisingly, such a position has led to numerous controversies. One of these occurred at the 1986 World Championships, where the UCI banned a United States bike at the starting line. Despite having seen the bike at the Goodwill Games and having awarded its rider the world record just eleven days earlier, the UCI disqualified the design, claiming the fairings served only aerodynamic purposes. The ensuing controversy was both technical and political. Armed with X-rays, the frame builder argued his case by claiming the seat tube would collapse without the fairings, making them functional as well as aerodynamic. Ed Burke, the U.S. Cycling Federation Director of Sports Medicine, Science, and Technology, argued that the Russian and French bikes had gussetted bottom brackets for purely aerodynamic reasons, yet their bikes were permitted.[17] Politically, the American team felt cheated. The UCI had seen and permitted the bike previously; outlawing it on the starting line put the team at an extreme disadvantage.

Ideally, the UCI would preserve the tradition and challenge of cycling by fairly and objectively regulating technological innovations. In reality, however, the task is next to impossible without a coherent definition of cycling, and therein lies the essential challenge. Manufacturers and federations cannot comply with the rules without understanding them. Banning an innovation one year and accepting it another, prohibiting a bike in one race and allowing it in another, only serve to confuse. Preserving the challenge and tradition of cycling is an important goal, but ad hoc regulations can frequently compromise the integrity of the sport.

Nonconforming Golf Clubs. The design of the putter head invites innovation as it is extremely difficult to putt accurately and up to 40 percent of scoring may depend on the golfer's ability to do so. Because the impact at which the putter hits the ball occurs at such a low speed, the USGA has allowed a good deal of creative play in their design. For all the innovations in form and material that have been allowed, however, much has been disqualified. The catalog of nonconforming putters includes objects of whimsy, eccentricity, and at times, undeniable beauty.

ABOVE: Putter with a mirror, considered an artificial device. Designer: Bruce Hazelton, 1993. Courtesy USGA, Far Hills, NJ

Athletic Challenge: Golf Balls

In addition to preserving sporting tradition, sports organizations ban technological innovations to protect athletic challenge. Bernard Suits, an eloquent and humorous sport and games philosopher, defines games as activities requiring inefficient means to accomplish a goal for which the means and ends are inseparable and the inefficiencies are accepted purely for the sake of the activity they make possible.[18] In other words, although it would be more efficient to carry the dimpled white ball and place it into the hole, golfers stand hundreds of yards away and hit it with a long club. Golfers accept these inefficiencies not because ethics require them or the law mandates them, but because such inefficient means create the test they want to take.

Golfers enjoy the game not just for the camaraderie and fresh air, but also for its test of skills:

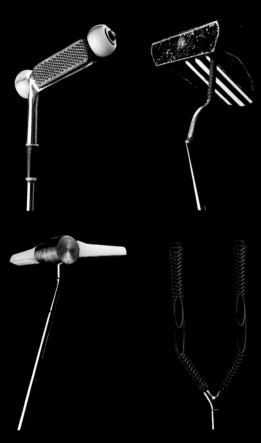

UPPER LEFT: Putter with wheels—moving parts violate a rule that all parts of the club be fixed. Designer: William Girrbach, 1993

UPPER RIGHT: Putter with rear flange that protrudes at a 45 degree angle. Designer: Jay Perkins, 1989

LOWER LEFT: L-shaped putter head. Designer: William Girrbach, 1993

LOWER RIGHT: Putter with a wishbone-shaped shaft containing dual handles. Designer: Ed Holbus, 1994.

Courtesy USGA, Far Hills, NJ

using a long club to drive a small ball into an only slightly larger hole hundreds of yards away requires driving distance and accuracy, as well as putting precision. A golf ball with a guidance system guaranteeing a hole-in-one on every shot would eliminate the challenge of the game.

While preserving the challenge of golf might require banning certain innovations, prohibiting all innovations would limit the test of skills. Throughout the history of the game, the design of the golf ball has demonstrated this paradox. Innovations in ball design have made more durable and cost effective equipment. Fourteenth-century golfers used a "feathery," a hand-sewn cowhide shell stuffed with a handful of boiled feathers.[19] Artisan ball makers could complete only four or five per day, and lung diseases from inhaling feathers ended their careers early. Moreover, the hand-sewn balls would split after a few uses or under rainy conditions. The low supply and high demand for the feathery balls created a price out of the range for all but the wealthiest aristocrats.[20]

Gutta-percha or "guttie" balls provided a less expensive and sturdier alternative. Legend has it that in 1843 a St. Andrews University professor and avid golfer received a statue packed in gutta-percha shavings that he then heated and formed into a ball (gutta-percha is a plastic substance formed from the latex of certain Malaysian trees). Although the ball began to dominate golf courses throughout Scotland, it demanded aerodynamic refinement. The smooth surface did not offer the distance or predictability golfers required. Golf aficionados noticed that worn balls, with nicks and scratches, soared farther and were aerodynamically superior to new balls. The demand for worn balls led manufacturers to hand hammer abrasions into the new ball. Manufacturing refinements replaced this laborious process with molds producing grooved, dimpled, or pimpled balls.[21]

The development and growth in rubber materials led to a bouncier ball, known as the Haskell ball. In 1899, while meeting an acquaintance at the Goodrich Rubber Company, Coburn Haskell thought of making a bouncier golf ball by wrapping rubber thread around a rubber core.[22] Today's three-piece ball construction differs only minimally from that of the Haskell. The cover rubbers have become more durable as balata (a plastic formed from the milk of the bully tree) has replaced gutta-percha. Surlyn, a synthetic manufactured by DuPont, provides an even sturdier alternative for the recreational player. The three-piece ball of the weekend hacker has a thick rubber tape—which breaks less and is faster to wind—wrapped around the core instead of the rubber thread used for premium balls. In the seventies, Spalding offered a two-piece ball with only a core and cover that was both inexpensive and durable. Elite golfers, however, preferred the "feel" of the three-piece ball with the less durable balata cover. Between the thirties and seventies, golf balls, regardless of construction, looked virtually identical. The pattern of 336 symmetrical hemispherical dimples was easy to manufacture, even if it was not ideal for performance.

The Haskell ball magnified the revolution in golf initiated by the guttie ball, which required courses to expand their holes to accommodate the longer flight ball and the growth in participant numbers. Some course architects added bunkers and water hazards to increase the premium on accuracy, emphasizing that driving distance was not the only skill golf tested. Women and seniors enjoyed the longer game the ball innovations provided—because they could drive the ball farther, they could compete at a more advanced level. Reductions in

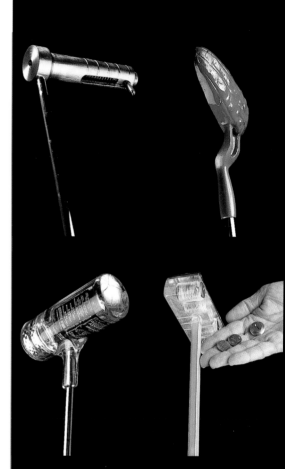

UPPER LEFT: Putter head with spring. Designer: William Girrbach, 1993

UPPER RIGHT: Pickle-shaped putter with a fork-like neck. Designer: Ken Matzie, 1991

LOWER LEFT: Jack Daniels putter that contains liquid, violating the ban on moving parts. Designer: Ray Florian, 1990

LOWER RIGHT: The weight of this clear plastic putter can be adjusted using ordinary coins. Because the adjustment is internal, within the head, and because the putter has no moving parts, it was approved by the USGA. Designer: Ray Florian, 1990

Courtesy USGA, Far Hills, NJ

ABOVE LEFT: Iron club with neck positioned on back of head. Designer: Fred Deutsch

ABOVE RIGHT: Putter with two mirrors in the head—one is set at a 45-degree angle, the other positioned horizontally to reflect to the golfer's eye. Mirrors, deemed artificial devices, are banned. Designer: Michael McCusker.

Courtesy USGA, Far HIlls, NJ

FACING PAGE: **Polara Plus Golf Ball (1974).** In the words of designer Fred Holstrom, "The Polara Plus was designed with the weekend golf hacker in mind, [delivering] a 50 percent improvement in directional performance." Only about half the ball, the surface at its "equator," was covered with dimples. Toward the poles of the ball dimples are more shallow or are filled in entirely. The so-called "Happy Non-Hooker" made for a more accurate—if shorter playing—ball. Courtesy Fred Holstrom

ball costs also opened the game to a wider range of social classes, though not races. And as so often happens in the technology of sports equipment, one innovation engendered another: more durable clubs were needed to hit the harder new balls. Hickory shafts yielded to harder woods, to steel, and then to graphite and titanium.

The golfing revolution concerned traditionalists and the United States Golf Association (USGA), the governing body for the sport in the U.S. and Mexico. To address some of their concerns, the USGA banned steel shafted clubs in 1922, only to rescind the ban in 1926.[23] Golf ball innovations, however, continued to "plague" the sport. By the seventies, ball manufacturers had begun to experiment with and patent different dimple patterns to provide a greater aerodynamic advantage. Manufacturers produced balls with larger, shallower dimples; with fewer dimples; with dimples of a different shape; and with hundreds of added dimples. The science of golf ball manufacture, design, and testing began to create balls that could travel distances that some feared would make existing courses obsolete. Moreover, such balls might eliminate the hours of practice necessary to perfect the swing required to send a ball hundreds of yards. The USGA did not support the notion of players buying their shots in a pro shop.

In response, the USGA has adopted an overall distance standard. This allows manufacturers maximum flexibility and creativity in the design, materials, and construction of balls, but restricts the distance they can travel.[24] The Golf Ball Manufacturers Association (GBMA) fought USGA regulation, arguing that innovation and distance were the chief selling points of their products. The USGA compromised by allowing all balls then existing and establishing a negotiated tolerance range.[25] The rule prohibited balls from exceeding 280 yards when hit with the USGA's Iron Byron ball testing machine.[26]

Since the USGA and manufacturers focused on distance, two scholars sought to design a better golf ball by focusing, instead, on accuracy. Fred Holmstrom, a physicist at San Jose State Univer-

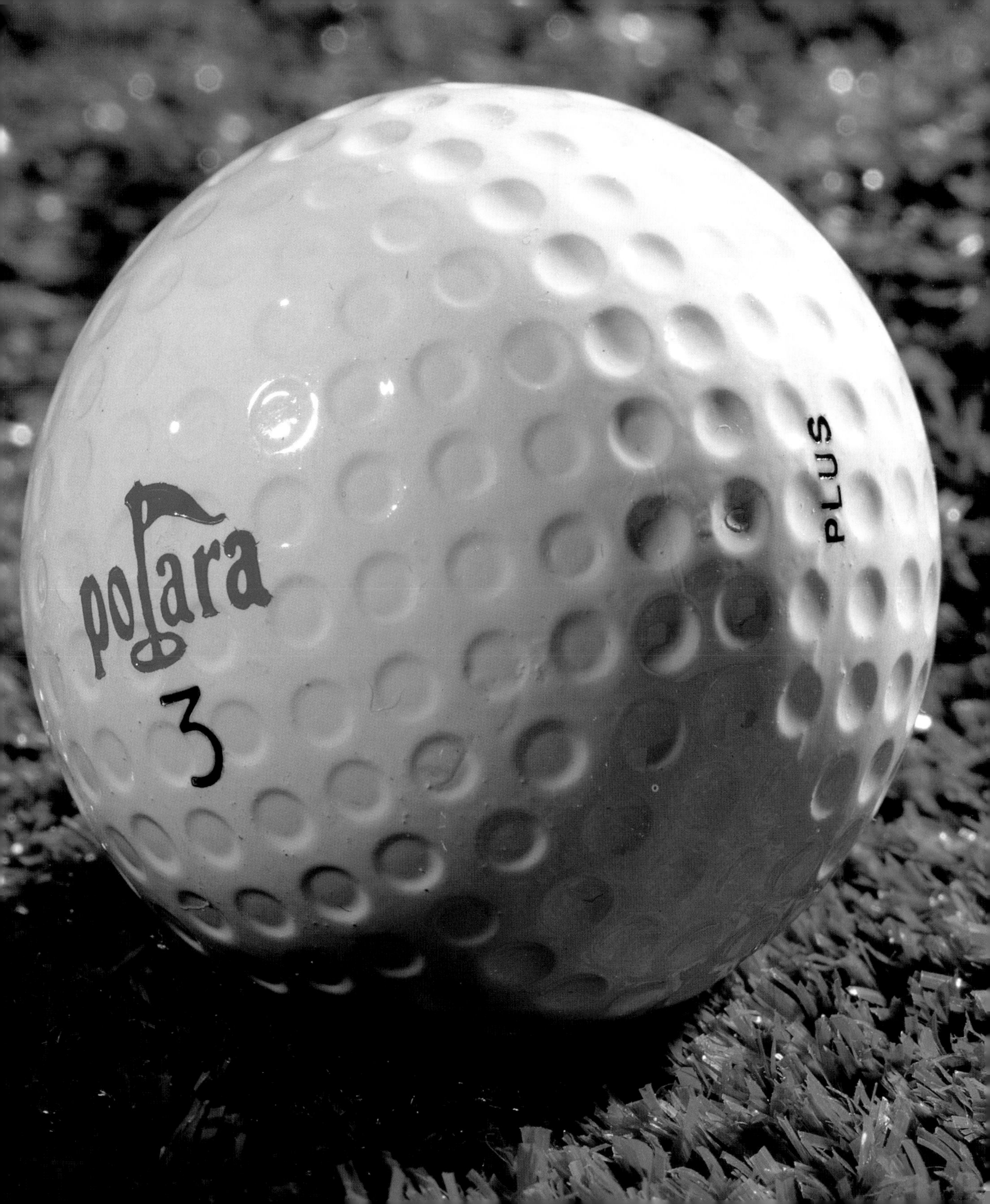
polara
3
PLUS

sity, and Daniel Nepela, an IBM chemist, were working together on a semiconductor project when a 1949 article in the *Journal of Applied Physics* on the aerodynamics of the golf ball caught their attention. They were most interested in the issues related to the balance of lift and drag forces on smooth and dimpled balls at different rotational speeds. Though not golfers themselves, the two scientists became intrigued by the aerodynamic and design challenge of a better golf ball. The Polara ball was the fruit of their investigations.[27]

Holmstrom and Nepela set out to minimize the age-old problems plaguing most golfers: the hook and the slice, problems longer balls exacerbated. To increase accuracy, they abandoned the traditional symmetrical dimple pattern. Their theoretical experimentation suggested that if the dimples on the poles were shallower than those on the circumference, a gyroscopic effect would produce a ball resistant to hooks and slices, reducing curvature as much as 75 percent. To test this theory, they created prototypes by modifying traditional golf balls. Balls were sanded down so that the rubber cement that filled the dimples would not yield an over-weight ball; dimples were then filled individually—some completely and others only minimally, creating a range of balls from those basically identical to the traditional ball to those virtually smooth.[28]

A golf pro at San Jose State University tested the prototypes by intentionally imparting a hook or a slice on the ball, and their theory proved correct. The more radical the design, the smoother the polar regions, the more resistant to hooks or slices the ball became.[29] A trade-off existed, however, with regard to distance. The less accurate the ball, the farther it would fly. Content with the test, Holmstrom and Nepela applied for and received a patent for the Polara in 1974. When the press and the USGA learned of the new ball, the "happy non-hooker" divided the golfing community.

Predictably, the USGA was concerned that the new technology would minimize the challenge of golf. It feared that golfers would no longer have to perfect their swing with practice or lessons, but could purchase a technological fix yielding accurate drives. The USGA requested the inventors bring their balls to the USGA testing facility for evaluation using both mechanical and human golfers. Although the tests showed other balls to be as accurate as the Polara, the unusual flight pattern of the ball continued to disturb USGA officials. The Polara seemed to "self-correct" in flight. From these tests, the USGA concluded the innovative ball, though meeting all existing specifications, would be detrimental to the game.

The logistics of banning a ball that conforms to all written requirements remains a simpler task than banning an innovative club: the USGA simply publishes a list of balls approved for play. Without providing a specific reason for omitting the Polara from the list, the ball was proscribed by omission. By contrast, a club might remain legal until the USGA specifically excludes it.

Bringing their case to court, the makers of the Polara argued that if the USGA was concerned that their innovation compromised the integrity of golf, then it should establish a performance standard; they were confident that their ball could meet any such standard, that their radical design actually reduced the distance the ball traveled, leaving golfers to negotiate a trade-off between distance and accuracy. This trade-off, they noted, would preserve the challenge of golf. The USGA agreed that a performance standard would address legitimate concerns, but claimed that the implementation of such a standard was not feasible.[30]

Indeed, after mechanical tests failed to yield accurate information, and human tests provided an inadequate basis for a performance standard (while machines can consistently replicate a given motion, humans prove much less consistent), in 1977 the USGA sought a standard based on form or design—as opposed to performance—the "symmetry rule." By 1981, the official standard was published and enforced: "The ball must not be designed, manufactured or intentionally modified to have flight properties which differ from those of a spherically symmetrical ball."[31] When the USGA was concerned about the distance balls traveled, it had initiated a performance standard. The case of ball accuracy might be philosophically identical to the case of ball distance, but practically they were very different.

This symmetry standard failed to protect the so-called integrity of golf in several ways. First, it prohibited an innovation that may not have minimized the challenge of golf. Because the Polara patent was flexible and a trade-off existed between accuracy and distance, many of the Polara designs would not have allowed golfers to "buy" their swings. Instead, it would have allowed some golfers to spend more time on the links practicing their skills rather than searching for balls in the woods. Highly skilled golfers would have reaped no advantage from it, as they tend to be more accurate and are unwilling to compromise the distance of their shots. More importantly, the symmetry standard opened the door for innovative designers to improve accuracy and compromise the challenge of the sport, so long as the dimple pattern was symmetrical. Since the USGA couldn't anticipate all the potential design innovations manufacturers might try to improve accuracy, they would have better protected their sport by establishing performance criteria.

Tennis Equipment

The tennis community faced similar challenges of innovation when a new stringing pattern challenged the sport's tradition. Tennis technology policy began with specifications for court dimensions and balls. In 1914 the International Lawn Tennis Federation (ILTF), the predecessor to the International Tennis Federation (ITF), authorized tennis balls for use in tournaments.[32] For the 1924 Olympic Games in Paris, the ILTF selected an American manufactured ball. This decision enraged the French Tennis Association, which threatened to withdraw from competition on their own soil.[33] Their fury did not stem simply from national pride; it was the result of a technical concern. Despite specifications for ball size, weight, and bounce, different compression in balls made some feel heavier and others lighter. American balls felt lighter; Europeans were used to the heavier. This controversy led to a standard compression requirement for tennis balls effective 1 January 1926.[34]

In contrast to the regulation of tennis balls, there was no restriction on racket innovation from the sixteenth century until 1978, though royal tennis enthusiasts of the Renaissance were critical of the new technology—the racket—in the first place. Playing tennis by hand had been considered excellent exercise. The racket, however, minimized effort, making the game more, and for some too, efficient. How rackets compromised the challenge of tennis was less important to the Renaissance elite than how the rackets destroyed the grace and elegance of the game. For both challenge and aesthetics, then, a small number of players continued to play *jeu de paume*.

Despite social pressure to play the traditional, challenging, and esthetic game, without a sanctioning body regulating equipment *jeu de paume* became a racket sport. This transformation began with players protecting their hands with gloves and then weaving rope around their hands, which eventually gave way to wooden paddles. By the beginning of the seventeenth century, outdoor courts brought the game to the middle classes, and the racket, strung with sheep intestines, into prominence. The first rackets were relatively short by modern standards, and manufacturers experimented with diagonal stringing patterns and asymmetric racket designs to "dig" the ball.[35] Tennis changed from a hand sport to a racket game as it moved from a purely elite to a middle-class sport. Ironically, today handball is a popular inner-city game, while tennis is traditionally considered a country-club sport.

The tennis racket changed little from the seventeenth century through World War II, after which revolutions in materials yielded powerful new rackets that transformed the game. Inspired by steel-shafted golf clubs, in 1965 René Lacoste, the French champion, patented a stainless steel racket frame that was both strong and light enough to generate creative new designs. Lacoste designed a racket with an open neck, reducing air resistance on the swing and weight in the hand. Lighter and more aerodynamically efficient, it allowed players to increase their swing velocity and thus the power of their shots. Jimmy Connors made this design famous and popular, playing with the Wilson 2000 in 1967.

Witnessing the success of Wilson's steel racket, Spalding marketed an aluminum version in 1968.[36] In that same year, Grand Slam tournaments became open to professionals, bringing an influx of money and interest to the sport. The growing number of recreational players provided the ideal market for these rackets, and they demanded the added power of new designs and materials. The

elite player, by contrast, preferred the feel of wood. But by the late seventies, composites of materials such as graphite and wood allowed manufacturers to produce rackets offering both power and feel.

While modified stringing systems and racket shapes appeared on the courts before the seventies, the nature of wood limited potentially revolutionary changes. Thus, for a hundred years, tennis rackets had retained a standard design. In 1885 a large-head racket did appear on the court, but the wood frame could not withstand the tension necessary to successfully string the racket.[37]

Oversized rackets arrived on the tennis scene in 1976 when a recreational tennis player, frustrated by his off-center shots, blamed his racket and decided to do something about it. As he had twenty years before, when frustration on the ski slopes led to a revolution in ski materials and manufacturing, Howard Head used his engineering ingenuity to design a racket that would increase his sporting success. He proceeded to design an oversized racket for the Prince company that would not twist uncontrollably when hit off center. This was accomplished by increasing the width of the racket face and improving its resistance to angular motion. The new shape quadrupled the size of the sweet spot and reduced the vibrations that caused tennis elbow.

As with the Polara golf ball, the oversized racket divided the community for which it was intended. While traditionalists and elite players reacted with skepticism, many weekend hackers snuck their new Prince rackets onto the courts. Those who enjoyed playing with the innovation acknowledged that the racket looked odd, while traditionalists admitted that the racket was perfectly legal. The rules of tennis included no definition of a tennis racket: one could use—and Bobby Riggs is said to have done so—a broom to play a match.

Regardless of its legality, the Prince large-head racket, according to many, did not look like a tennis racket. The *New York Times* said the racket lacked charisma: male players using it experienced a "definite loss of machismo" and female players a "loss of grace."[38] Aesthetically, the racket was a failure.

The larger head also seemed to serve as a substitute for skill and practice. Players wondered how one could miss any shot with such a large hitting surface. With the enlarged sweet spot, mediocre shots rebounded powerfully. Despite these perceived advantages, the racket did not immediately offer any benefits to the skilled player. Professionals, who hit off center less frequently than weekend hackers, would not trade accuracy for the larger sweet spot. And the oversized racket did compromise control: conventional stringing tensions were too low for its large and flexible frame, producing a severe trampoline effect. It took the introduction of a stiffer aluminum frame and a 20 percent increase in stringing tension to make the new racket truly revolutionary.

By the late seventies, the Prince oversized racket had initiated a tennis revolution. In 1978, Pam Shriver advanced to the U.S. Open final with her Prince racket, and Gene Mayer climbed from 148th in the world to fourth with the Prince.[39] By 1982, the hottest items on the Wimbledon court were oversized rackets, which Martina Navratilova described as the "'747s of the sport."[40] Such professional endorsements complemented a comprehensive marketing campaign. Prince actively marketed the racket to top junior players for whom it added needed power to still developing games. Seniors loved the racket because it gave them more power and extended their playing years. The racket revolutionized the game by eliminating the longer, fluid stroke in favor of shorter, choppier strokes and

placed a premium on an aggressive style of play.[41] For recreational, women, senior, and junior players, the new innovation complemented existing talents by providing added power and increasing the intensity, challenge, and popularity of the sport.

Throughout this period of innovation, the ITF continued to allow any and all racket innovations. This liberality ended in 1978 in response to an innovative stringing system known as "spaghetti strings." In the early 1970s, a Bavarian horticulturalist, Werner Fischer, developed the unique system, and while it was used in Germany in the mid-seventies, it didn't receive international notice until 1977.

Unlike the traditional stringing pattern, with a single set of main strings interwoven with a set of cross strings, the double-strung system had three planes of nonintersecting strings. On the strings was a protective plastic coating that was thought to resemble spaghetti—thus the name. This stringing system grabbed the ball, holding it on the strings longer and imparting more spin. While the United States Tennis Association argued in court that the stringing pattern imparted 30 to 60 percent more spin on the ball, an Italian laboratory studying its effects determined only that a ball hit with the racket rebounded irregularly and unpredictably.[42] Nevertheless, the top-spin strokes made possible by the racket invariably confused and defeated opponents.

The immediate impact of the spaghetti-stringing system was too dramatic and controversial for the ITF to ignore. In May of 1977, the Swiss Tennis Federation, concerned that two "humdrum" touring pros, France's Georges Goven and Germany's Erwin Muller, could upset favorites throughout Europe, requested the ITF look into the technology that many deemed responsible for Goven's and Muller's success.[43] Since the ITF had no rules governing rackets, the spaghetti-strung—or "double-strung"—

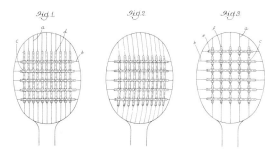

Spaghetti-String Racket (1977). Designed by Werner Fischer, the "spaghetti-string" racket's three planes of nonintersecting strings appeared to grab the ball, impart spin, and ultimately confuse and defeat opponents. TOP: Courtesy U.S. Patent Office. BOTTOM: Courtesy International Tennis Hall of Fame and Museum, Newport RI

nament, Ilie Nastase lost in the first round of a Paris Tournament to Goven and his new strings. A week after this frustrating defeat, Nastase appeared at the Aix-en-Provence tournament with a spaghetti-strung racket and beat Guillermo Vilas, who stormed off the court after losing a fifty-match win streak.[45] The fury over the racket led the ITF to institute a temporary ban on the racket in early October, only five months after first hearing of the new design.[46] This temporary ban led both to a permanent ban and a definition of the tennis racket—something missing from the rule book for centuries.

Although the ITF believed the racket compromised athletic challenge, the effects of the innovative stringing system were more complex. While the stringing pattern did impart more spin on the ball, the trade-off was a reduction in speed and power. Players began to hit more like Björn Borg—with heavy top spin—but less like Jimmy Connors, who hit hard, flat strokes. In other words, the technology did not benefit all players. It complemented those players who relied on top spin but had not mastered the skill, while detracting from the play of fast, power hitters like Connors. Many also believed that players like Borg, who hit high velocity top-spin shots, would improve little with the spaghetti stringing system. The degree to which the new technology compromised the challenge of the sport depended on the type of player and style of game.

Without more time and tests it would not become obvious whether the spaghetti-stringing system allowed players to buy victories at major tournaments. One *London Times* commentator cited novelty as the reason for the spaghetti string's initial success, reasoning that once players became familiar with the new stringing system, it's effect on the game would diminish: "Already there is evidence that players, initially baffled by the effect of

racket was considered legal. Dramatic upsets continued throughout the season as Michael Fishbach, ranked two hundredth by the Association of Tennis Professionals (ATP), upset both Billy Martin and sixteenth-seeded Stan Smith at the U.S. Open in September.[44] Unlike the Prince racket, the first public displays of the double-stringing system created huge upsets and appeared to replace natural talent and years of practice. Indeed, the racket turned mid-level professionals into champions.

The results of the U.S. Open in 1977 sent the established professional tennis elite into an uproar that the ITF could not ignore. Soon after that tour-the new stringing method can make the adjustment necessary to overcome it."[47]

Given this possibility, the manufacturer of the system lobbied for a trial period, arguing that it should be used for a year before its effect could be realistically evaluated. While such a trial period might have offered an ideal solution, as in the case of the Polara ball, it was not adopted. The ITF banned the spaghetti-strung racket by prohibiting tennis rackets from having non-intersecting strings and protrusions on the strings for performance purposes.

The majority of the tennis community supported the ITF's decision. Unlike the Prince racket, no significant segment of that community had developed a reliance or had a vested interest in the stringing system. Moreover, the revolutionary affects of the spaghetti-stringing system were immediate. It did not require manufacturing refinements and adjustments that might gradually yield a revolutionary impact. The gradual invasion of the large-head technology had allowed it to establish itself in the game before players could realize that it might compromise the integrity of the sport. Spaghetti strings, however, seemed to enable professional players to purchase their victories, rankings, and prize money. Despite the general consensus supporting the ITF, a few voiced opposition. The *Times* commentator offered his opinion: "The International Tennis Federation has panicked and made an ass of itself by the banning of what in my opinion was a seven-day wonder."[48] As new equipment enters the tennis arena, it will be incumbent upon the ITF to design a program to test and regulate technology—rather than to "panic" each time an invention enters the court.

Wild imaginations and engineering ingenuity will give rise to many new technologies that the ITF and other sports organizations will have to consider.

Presently, many shorter athletes are turning to longer rackets, equipment that can substitute for natural height and power. New composite materials and inventive stringing patterns result in an ever-increasing power game. To write effective technology policy for tennis, the ITF must consider how to balance sporting tradition, athletic challenge, and technological innovation.

Safety

Innovation in sports technology is often checked by concerns for safety. Two examples of this are the banning of both aerodynamic javelins and cone luge helmets. In the early eighties, engineers discovered that if the center of gravity of the javelin were shifted back, the improved javelin might soar farther than previously possible. Confirming this theory, Tom Petranoff set a new world record by over 20 meters using the redesigned javelin. For technique-oriented athletes, as opposed to physically strong athletes, the new technology helped realize victories and championships. So successful was the re-engineered javelin that it regularly flew beyond the allotted space in stadiums, landing in stands, and finally piercing a judges' tent at the 1984 Los Angeles Olympic Games. In 1986, the International Amateur Athletic Federation (IAAF), the governing body for track and field, banned the new aerodynamically designed javelin, requiring that its center of gravity be returned to its previous position to protect fans, participants, and judges.[49]

Although cone helmets would offer lugers an aerodynamic advantage, the Fédération Internationale de Luge de Course banned the helmets, which were significantly heavier than traditional helmets, and required an extended headrest solely for the purpose of balancing their oblong shape. Both the helmet's increased weight—which might result

**Cone-
Shaped
Luge Helmet.**
Though aerodynam-
ically advantageous,
cone-shaped luge helmets
were extremely heavy, a fact that raised
questions about their safety and led to their ban in
the late seventies. Courtesy Fédération Internationale
de Luge de Course

in neck injuries—and the possibility of the headrest
catching on the course or disrupting the balance of
the sled undermined its essential *raison d'être*:
safety. In response, the sport's governing body mandated a standard helmet shape for all athletes.[50]

Cost

The high cost of sports innovation may itself be
prohibitive. New technologies require extensive
research and development budgets. With many
countries unable to meet such expenses, sports
requiring high spending risk losing their participant
base and fan support. With this in mind, some
sports organizations have banned certain innovations to keep costs down. By setting strict limits on
the dimensions of legal kayaks, for example, the
governing body of kayaking believes it has slowed
down what were skyrocketing research and development costs.[51]

In rowing, sliding riggers designed to replace
the sliding seat in which the rower sits were
banned for similar financial reasons. The sliding
seat revolutionized rowing in the 1870s, turning the
choppy, upper-body sport into a graceful, full-
body activity. Although athletes had tried previously to incorporate their legs into the
rowing stroke by greasing their shorts or
sliding on the morning's oatmeal, rowing
had remained an upper-body exercise.
To send the shell cutting through water,
the rower faced the wake left behind
and came to the "catch" position. This
required leaning forward at the waist with
arms outstretched and oars poised above water.
Once at the catch position, the oarsmen would lift
his hands, thereby dropping the oar blades into the
water. The power drive would consist of swinging
the upper body back and bending the arms, bringing the oar handle into the stomach and propelling
the boat through the water. The sliding seat
allowed the rower to lengthen the power stroke
and take advantage of the powerful leg muscles.
Although the technique was more difficult to master, the added power increased speed and transformed the sport.

Despite the advantages of the sliding seat, it
remained an extremely inefficient system. Because
rowers faced the starting line rather than the finish
line, when they came to the catch they were moving
their whole body weight against the movement of
the shell. In an eight-man shell with athletes averag-
ing 200 pounds, 1,600 pounds would be moving
counter productively. To eliminate this problem, in
1972 an East Berliner, Klaus Filter, developed a sliding rigger. With this design the athlete's rear would
remain stationary while he pulled the foot stretch-
ers and rigger into the proper catch position. The

sliding rigger reduced drag and earned the Olympic single sculling gold in 1976. After the 1983 World Championships, in which all of the finalists were rowing in sliding rigger boats, sliding riggers were banned for reasons of cost.[52] Accepting the new design would necessarily have required all crews who wanted to stay competitive to purchase new shells. For the average college program—which required ten shells each for heavyweights, light-weights, and women—this cost would have been roughly $1.8 million.

Spectator Appeal

Technological decisions can change the nature of sports, including speed, balance of offense and defense, and aggression levels. By instituting such technologies as "shot clocks"—which demand an offensive attempt within a time limit—sports orga-nizations can speed up the action to meet fans' changing demands. Yet increased speed can also negatively impact fan interest. In 1952, an unknown Japanese player, Hiroshi Satoh, appeared at the Table Tennis World Championships with a racket covered with sponge rubber. Experimentation with rubber and padding as well as playing style led to a revolution in table tennis: the game became signifi-cantly faster and more complex. While at first these changes may have increased the interest in and challenge of table tennis, the game eventually became too fast for fans to follow; three-second ral-lies gave fans little time to get involved in a point. Due to these innovations, table tennis has become an offense-dominated game where elite players regularly miss what appear to be easy shots.[53]

To combat part of this problem, the governing body banned rackets with two different types of rubber with the same color. Table tennis paddles now must have two different colors, one on each side, so the opponent knows what type of rubber the incoming shot is hit with (the type of rubber determining to a large degree the characteristics of the shot). Some changes currently under considera-tion include making the ball either larger or softer, limiting the types of rubber used, or changing the rules that determine a legal serve. With regard to fan interest, the lack of attention paid to emerging technological innovations in 1952 has led to a need for new revisions in the sport today.[54]

In addition to game speed, sports organiza-tions must also consider how best to preserve image: today, how a sport appears on television has a good deal to do with its potential success. Muddy football players and dirty brown grass on fairways have little appeal on color television. Similarly, in 1994 the luge federation banned shinny plastified suits because commentators claimed the athletes looked like aliens. In the same year, the National Basketball Association banned shoes that lit on impact.

Especially offensive, however, were the tear-away jerseys used in collegiate football. Coaches often tell defensive players to grab anything to bring down the player running the ball. Part of any-thing would be the player's jersey. But what if instead of bringing down the ball carrier the defen-sive player was left with but a handful of cloth? The ball carrier would end up with more yards or even a touchdown, while the defender would be frustrated in his efforts, holding fabric. Fritz Crisler coached at Princeton in the early 1930 and claims to have lost a game when an opponent brought down his half-back by pulling on his player's jersey sleeve. To prevent such a replay, in 1947, when he coached at Michigan, his players dressed in tear-away jerseys; some went through thirty shirts in a single game.[55]

Charging the offending team a time out while the player changed, the NCAA required players to

Tear-Away Football Jersey (1969). Tear-away football jerseys, such as this version worn by Johnny Musso at the University of Alabama in 1969, prevented players from firmly grabbing one another during a tackle. Courtesy of Paul W. Bryant Museum, The University of Alabama

Sports organizations want to protect the integrity of their sports while encouraging growth. Doing so requires banning certain technologies while permitting others. Determining in which category a particular design might fall is difficult. The impact of some innovations cannot be understood until the sport has had a chance to adjust and the design of the new equipment has been refined: while aluminum baseball bats offered no advantage when they were first introduced, refinements in designs and alloys later created a performance-enhancing technology. Until table tennis players learned how to reap advantages from sponge rubber, the innovation did not dramatically alter the game. Technology has radically affected our games; keeping innovations in check will preserve sporting traditions and athletic challenge.

Sport is about gaining an advantage and testing human potential; yet dedication to preserving sporting challenge and tradition mandate an ambiguous relationship with new technologies. While innovations like the Polara golf ball and spaghetti-string racket advanced the efficiency of their respective games, they also compromised their challenges and traditions. Likewise, microwave ovens may facilitate cooking, but compromise traditional family rituals of meal preparation. How we choose technologies that will enrich our lives without compromising the traditions we cherish remains a predicament in the late twentieth century; and how such choices are addressed in the realm of sport may give us some direction for how we resolve them elsewhere in our lives.

sit out for a play while they changed their shirts on the sidelines. The NCAA's primary concern may have been cost. Some schools were spending $10,000 annually on tear-away jerseys, which, according to John Adams, then chair of the football rules committee, gave wealthier schools an unfair advantage. More problematic, however, was that the torn jerseys left shoulder pads exposed, minimizing their protective value. Finally, like slip-over vests, torn jerseys simply looked bad. For reasons of safety, cost, image, and fair play, the NCAA banned tear-away jerseys in 1982.[56]

Notes

1. John D. Allen, "History of Professional Baseball Rule Changes (1800–1972)" (Master's thesis, University of Wisconsin, 1971), 55.

2. Babe Ruth began his career wielding a 54-ounce bat, but hit his sixty home runs in 1927 with a 40-ounce club. Modern bats typically weigh 32 ounces. Steven Ashley, "Getting Good Wood (Or Aluminum) on the Ball," *Mechanical Engineering* (October 1990): 46.

3. Peter Gammons, "End of an Era," *Sports Illustrated*, 24 July 1989, 20.

4. Ibid.

5. Hank Hersch, "The Good Wood," *Sports Illustrated*, 14 April 1986, 79.

6. Gammons, "End of an Era," 18.

7. Ashley, "Getting Good Wood," 47.

8. Ted Brindenthal, telephone interview with the author, 30 January 1997. Brindenthal is NCAA staff liaison to the NCAA Baseball Rules Committee.

9. Ibid.

10. Ibid.

11. "Dimples Give Batters More Power," *Science News* 145, no. 22 (28 May 1994): 352.

12. *1997 NCAA Baseball Rules* (Overland Park, KS: National Collegiate Athletic Association, 1997), 21.

13. Steven Ashley, "Wood-Composite Baseball Bats Take the Field," *Mechanical Engineering* (August 1991): 43–45.

14. Matthew E. Mantell, "What is the UCI?" *Bicycling* 30, no. 5 (1989).

15. Union Cycliste Internationale (UCI), press release, Lausanne, Switzerland, 8 October 1996.

16. Ibid.

17. "Pursuit Bikes Rejected," *Velo News*, 14 November 1986.

18. Bernard Suits, *The Grasshopper: Games, Life, and Utopia* (Toronto: University of Toronto Press, 1978).

19. Susan Van Tijn, "In Search of the Perfect Golf Ball," *Financial Post Magazine,* February 1977, 10.

20. John Stuart Martin, *The Curious History of the Golf Ball* (New York: Horizon Press, 1968), 31.

21. Anthony Chase, "A Slice of Golf," *Science* 81 (July/August 1981): 90.

22. N. R. Kleinfeld, "In Pursuit of the Perfect Golf Ball," *New York Times*, 16 February 1986.

23. "Stymie Restored, Steel Shafts Out," *New York Times*, 6 April 1922.

24. "Distance Standard Set for Golf Balls," *New York Times*, 14 March 1976.

25. *Polara Enterprises Inc vs. United States Golf Association and Golf Ball Manufacturers Association,* transcript, United States District Court for the Northern District of California, 1984, book 1, 59–61.

26. As of 1995 the rules of golf maintain the 6 percent tolerance. *1995 Rules of Golf* (Far Hills, NJ: United States Golf Association, 1995).

27. John M. Davies, "The Aerodynamics of Golf Balls," *Journal of Applied Physics* 20, no. 9 (September 1949): 821–28.

28. *Polara Enterprises Inc vs. United States Golf Association,* 92-96; Ken Denlinger, "Polara Keeps the Golf Ball on Line, but Guilt Feelings Put It Off Course," *Washington Post*, 25 July 1977.

29. Fred Holmstrom, telephone interview with the author, 31 January 1995.

30. *Polara Enterprises Inc vs. United States Golf Association,* 124–25.

31. *Rules of Golf*, 110.

32. "Make of Tennis Balls," *New York Times*, 11 May 1914.

33. "Muhr Quits French Tennis Federation: Secretary Resigns After Conflict Over Choice of American Ball for Olympics." *New York Times*, 22 February 1924.

34. "Tennis World Aims at Standard Ball: Prevalence of International Matches Proves Need of Greater Uniformity," *New York Times*, 22 December 1924.

35. Parke Cummings, *American Tennis: The Story of a Game and Its People* (Boston, MA: Little Brown & Co., 1957), 170–71.

36. Steve Fiott "Frames of Reference," in *Racket Almanac* (Newport, RI: International Tennis Hall of Fame, n.d.), 22.

37. J. Parmley Paret, *Lawn Tennis* (New York: Macmillan Co., 1904); see photo with caption "Three of the 'Freak' Models," between pp. 78–79.

38. Holcomb B. Noble, "Secret Weapon or Barn Door?" *New York Times Magazine*, 21 November 1976, 58.

39. "Update: Pam and Her Prince," *Baltimore Magazine*, November 1978, 17.

40. Neil Amdur, "Big Racquets Are Hot Items," *New York Times*, 2 July 1982.

41. Robert J. LaMarche, "How the Prince Patent Has Changed the Game," *Tennis*, April 1986, 114.

42. Sport Allma, "Comparative Study between Traditional Stringing and Fischer Stringing," study prepared for the International Tennis Federation, n.d., 16.

43. J. D. Reed, "A Weighty Matter of Spaghetti and Tennis Balls," *Sports Illustrated*, 3 April 1978, 36.

44. "USTA Joins Double-Strung Racquet Ban," *New York Times*, 20 October 1977.

45. Alexander McNab, "Unraveling the Spaghetti Racket," *Tennis USA*, December 1977, 29.

46. "Spaghetti Racquet Banned," *New York Times*, 2 October 1977.

47. John Ballantine, "A Mark of Class," *Sunday Times* (London), 16 October 1977.

48. Ibid.

49. David Bjerklie, "High-Tech Olympians," *Technology Review* 96, no. 1 (January 1993): 29–30.

50. Fred Zimney, telephone interview with the author, October 1996. Zimney was a member of the United States Luge Association.

51. Bjerklie, "High-Tech Olympians," 29–30.

52. Christopher Dodd, *The Story of World Rowing* (London: Stanley Paul, 1992), 108–9.

53. Rufford Harris, letter to the author, 30 October 1996.

54. Ibid.

55. Marshall Smith, "The Specialist," *Time*, 3 November 1947, 72–76.

56. "New NCAA Rules Designed to Improve Safety of Uniforms," *Athletic Purchasing and Facilities* (April 1981): 27–29.

Contributors

Akiko Busch has written about architecture, design, and craft for the last seventeen years, and her work appears regularly in publications in these fields, among them *Architectural Record*, *Graphis*, *ID*, and *Print*. She is currently a contributing editor at both *Metropolis* and *House & Garden* magazines. Her most recent book, *Rooftop Architecture: The Art of Going Through the Roof*, was published by Henry Holt in 1991.

J. Nadine Gelberg earned her Master's Degree in History at Pennsylvania State University and wrote her thesis on the plastic football helmet. She completed her Ph.D in the Department of Kinesiology at Penn State with a dissertation on sport technology policy.

Candace Lyle Hogan has written extensively about sports as a syndicated columnist, associate editor for *womenSports* magazine, and managing editor of *The Runner* and *Sports Inc*. She is currently a freelance writer and editor and is at work on a history of women's sports.

Steven Skov Holt has been a designer at Smart Design, editor of *ID* magazine, and co-founder of the product design department at the Parsons School of Design. Since 1995, he has been chair of the industrial design program at the California College of Arts and Crafts in San Francisco. He is also currently director of strategy at frogdesign in Sunnyvale, California, and takes on occasional graphic and industrial design projects.

Steven Langehough, guest curator, has been with the Cooper-Hewitt, National Design Museum since 1979. As associate registrar, he is responsible for mounting temporary and traveling exhibitions. He received his M.F.A. from Cranbrook Art Academy. An avid sports fan, Langehough coaches youth soccer.

Diana Nyad set the record for longest swim in history in 1979, when she swam nonstop 102.5 miles from the Bahamas to Florida, and was inducted into the National Women's Sports Hall of Fame in 1986. She has written two books—*Other Shores* and *Basic Training*—and, as an announcer with ABC's *Wide World of Sports* from 1980 to '88, she covered three Olympic games and dozens of events around the globe. Currently, she hosts documentaries on the Outdoor Life network and presents a regular column on National Public Radio's *Morning Edition*.